RAISIN WINE

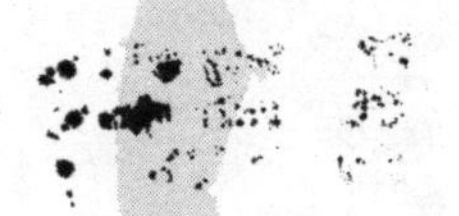

RAISIN

A BOYHOOD IN A DIFFERENT MUSKOKA

James Bartleman

A DOUGLAS GIBSON BOOK

McCLELLAND & STEWART

Hardcover edition published 2007
Trade paperback edition published 2008

Library and Archives Canada Cataloguing in Publication

Bartleman, James, 1939-
Raisin wine : a boyhood in a different Muskoka / James Bartleman.

"Douglas Gibson books".
ISBN 978-0-7710-1140-5 (bound). – ISBN 978-0-7710-1264-8 (pbk.)

1. Bartleman, James, 1939- – Childhood and youth. 2. Chippewas of Mnjikaning First Nation – Biography. 3. Muskoka (Ont. : District municipality) – Biography. I. Title.

FC636.B37A3 2007 971.3'160492 C2006-904212-8

We acknowledge the financial support of the Government of Canada through the Book Publishing Industry Development Program and that of the Government of Ontario through the Ontario Media Development Corporation's Ontario Book Initiative. We further acknowledge the support of the Canada Council for the Arts and the Ontario Arts Council for our publishing program.

Typeset in Dante by M&S, Toronto
Printed and bound in Canada

A Douglas Gibson Book

This book is printed on acid-free paper that is 100% recycled, ancient-forest friendly (100% post-consumer recycled).

McClelland & Stewart Ltd.
75 Sherbourne Street
Toronto, Ontario
M5A 2P9
www.mcclelland.com

1 2 3 4 5 12 11 10 09 08

For my parents, Maureen and Percy Bartleman.

Acknowledgements

I should like to thank my wife, Marie-Jeanne, my son Alain, as well as Douglas Gibson and Nanda Casucci-Byrne.

"We live our life as the tale is told."

– Psalm 90

Contents

ONE

—

Voices in the Wind

THEY LIVED IN A THREE-ROOM, two-storey house on a one-acre lot overgrown with trees in Port Carling, a small village in Ontario's cottage country. The mother, who was Indian, had long been familiar with the dwelling. As a child in the 1920s and 1930s, she had spent time with her extended family in the tiny local enclave known as the Indian Camp where native people from her distant reserve gathered in the summers to fish and to sell handicrafts to tourists. In those early days, she used to cross the street whenever she approached it, for a villager had hanged himself on a backyard apple tree and it was rumoured that his tormented spirit had taken up residence in the long-deserted house.

Certainly the building gave every impression of being haunted. Their glass shattered by stones thrown by schoolchildren over the years, two large windows stared down at passersby on the street like the Windigo, sinister eater of human flesh and evil spirit in Chippewa mythology – at least in the imagination of the impressionable native child who had heard too many tales of monsters at home for comfort. Her fear was that the resident ghost would float out of one of the black and eyeless sockets to seize her and do her in. She never dreamed that one day the house would become her home.

During the Great Depression, the Indian girl, now a young woman, married a white man, a hard-working unskilled labourer, scarcely older than herself. And other than a fondness for home-brew (raisin wine was his favourite), he was a good husband. After their initial shock, for white men did not marry Indians in those days, his parents accepted their Indian daughter-in-law. The war came. The army rejected the husband because of a bad heart. The mixed couple, with their growing brood of half-breed children, drifted from town to town until they arrived in the village of her youth the year after the war ended. Their children were now four in number and the family lived in a tent on wasteland near the dump for the summer and in an uninsulated summer cottage for the winter. Desperate for a home of her own, the mother remembered the abandoned house.

The years had not been kind to it. Now known in the village as "the old shack on the hill," it had neither indoor toilet nor electricity. Likewise, rainwater leaked through the much-patched tarpaper roof, the wooden pillars that served as foundations were rotting away, and the house leaned perilously to one side. But the unpainted, weather-beaten exterior walls that had turned barnwood-black with age were solid, the walls of the one room occupying the ground floor were clean, and the partitions of deep-brown hemlock studs covered by thin boards separating the two upstairs bedrooms were clean and dry. The mother shrugged off her fears of the Windigo, persuaded the owners to let her purchase the property by making small monthly payments, and moved her family into the new home in the spring of 1947.

The mother may have put the story of the hanged man and ghost behind her, but her son, to whom she had confided the story, had not. Not that he was really afraid. He was, after all, seven years old and had been told by his father that ghosts did not exist. Nonetheless, he was never at ease at night when he had to visit the outdoor privy some distance behind the old house in a grove of sumach trees. In fact, anyone, even someone with a less active imagination than the boy's, would have found the experience spooky. Flashlights were a luxury the family could not afford, and the boy's only source of light as he stumbled along the path was from coal-oil lamps inside the house that filtered out through the ancient single-pane windows casting eerie shadows on the ground outside. To make matters worse, the boy was convinced that he could hear ghostly moaning sounds whenever he passed the apple tree where the neighbour had hanged himself. His unease turned to fear on moonlit nights since at times he thought he saw the victim, a rope around his neck, swinging in the obscurity among the branches of the apple tree. And his fear turned to terror on pitch-dark windy ones since the moaning from the restless spirit then seemed to reach new levels of despair.

Once back inside the house, the boy felt brave – at least in the company of his family when it gathered together in the evenings before going to bed. There was safety in numbers in that crowded room serving as kitchen, dining room, and living room. A wood-burning cookstove, a supply of drying wood, and a sink occupied one half of the space. A row of rubber boots was neatly lined up just inside the front door. Behind the stove, screwed into the wall, were rows of clothes hooks holding the coats and hats of the family members. An oilcloth-covered kitchen table, six hardwood maple chairs ordered from Eaton's catalogue, and an old couch filled the other half. Off in a corner was the icebox with its two standard compartments –

one for milk, butter, meat and vegetables and the other for blocks of ice, cut out of Lake Muskoka in the dead of winter and delivered door-to-door throughout the year by a local farmer.

In addition to the boy, a crying baby, a quarrelsome younger sister, a bossy older brother, an overworked mother, and a preoccupied father filled every available space. This did not include a dog and cat who cohabited reluctantly with a baby raccoon the father had rescued and which he was raising with more open affection than he gave to his own children. The clamour was such, the boy reassured himself, that the ghost in the apple tree, if it really existed, would never dare enter the house.

Upstairs in bed, when the other family members were asleep, he was not so certain. Despite the comforting presence of his brother and sisters in their shared bedroom, the boy was worried. For when the house was silent, he thought he could hear the sounds of the moaning from the afflicted soul through the old building's exterior walls. Having heard his parents say that death by suicide was unnatural, the boy thought the spectre must be guilt-ridden at having taken his own life.

And deepening his anxiety, he was preoccupied by a story of an encounter with supernatural evil told in all sincerity by a cousin of his mother. This cousin, a quiet

Indian trapper with dark brown skin and piercing black eyes, often came to the house to spend the evening with the family bearing carcasses of beaver and muskrat as gifts for the mother to cook. On a recent visit, he had been more taciturn than usual and had looked so often at the window and with such a deeply troubled expression, the boy's mother had asked him what was wrong.

Speaking in a barely audible voice, the cousin confessed that despite being warned repeatedly by the preacher on his reserve that gambling was wicked, he had played cards for money late into the night at the home of a neighbour. Outside, it was a cold, dark, moonless night. Inside, six friends sat around the kitchen table, illuminated by a solitary coal-oil lamp whose thin yellow glow reflected off the glass of the bare windows, devoid of curtains and blinds. Four were playing and two were watching and waiting their turn to join in.

Along one wall in the shadows was a bench and on the bench were the coats of the guests along with a dipper and a pail of fresh, cold drinking water drawn from the well and carried in earlier in the evening by the host. A box of leghold traps was stuffed in the corner together with a pair of snowshoes. The room was comfortably warm, heated by a fire in a huge and ancient box stove centred on the worn linoleum covering the floor. Beside the stove was a wooden box filled with dry white birch firewood. The mellow scent of roll-your-own cigarettes and chewing tobacco blended comfortably with the smell of woodsmoke leaking from cracks in the cast-iron firebox and with the odours that lingered in the room from the family dinner earlier in the evening: fried whitefish, boiled potatoes, and bannock, the traditional Indian flatbread eaten with every meal.

On another wall, barely visible in the dim light, was a large sepia-tinged photograph in a standard military-issue picture frame of the host's brother, smartly dressed in full military uniform. The Canadian Army had provided similar photographs of new recruits to their families in the Great War – as the First World War was known in those days – and proud parents across Canada had hung them in places of prominence in their homes. There were many such pictures on the reserve. More than a quarter of a century earlier, the young man in the picture and the men playing cards that night – together with almost all the eligible men from the community, including the boy's great-grandfather – had travelled to the closest town and enrolled in the Canadian Army. From there they were shipped to the huge Camp Borden military base for basic training and then by fast troop transports to

England, and on to the trenches of the Western Front.

The culture shock had been enormous. Teenagers and men whose first language was Chippewa and who had spent their lives in the bush or on the lakes as trappers and fishermen were thrown together with white farmers, factory hands, office workers, private schoolboys, and British immigrants, most of whom had never met a native person. In short order, the native soldiers proved themselves as snipers and forward artillery observers, even transmitting coordinates back to the guns in their native languages to foil German code-breakers seeking to intercept Allied battlefield communications. For the duration of the war, at least, the natives were treated as equals, and bonded with their white compatriots.

Many of the native recruits, including the young man in the picture, had lost their lives in showers of mud and steel during the numberless battles of the war in Northern France and in Belgian Flanders. The others, some shattered in body and spirit, had come home to get on with their lives and to grow old. Now the picture of the young Indian soldier, frozen in time but with eyes that met and followed visitors around the house, languished largely forgotten on the wall. And when from time to time the host opened the lid of the stove and threw in a stick of white birch firewood, the paper-thin bark covering would burst into flame with a flash of light that cast the shadows of the players onto the photograph of the long-dead soldier, who looked out at his former comrades-in-arms with deep, brooding melancholy.

The mood in the room was subdued, but there was an ample supply of raisin wine to drink and the card players were enjoying themselves trading jokes in the soft tones of their mother tongue. Suddenly the cousin sensed the presence of something vile and corrupt. He glanced at the window and was horrified to see the devil, horns, tail, and all, peering in and smiling. Satan, the trapper was convinced, was showing his satisfaction at catching sinners whose immortal souls, after the death of their bodies, he would drag, screaming and pleading for mercy, down to hell. And in hell – according to the Bible-thumping preacher who loved nothing better than to frighten his charges in his weekly sermons by quoting from the Book of Revelations – they would suffer fire, brimstone, and untold miseries throughout eternity.

The cousin shouted a warning to the others before dashing coatless out the door and fleeing to his own house. He had a distinguished record fighting overseas and was not easily spooked. But he nevertheless swore that he would rather return to artillery barrages, hand-to-hand combat in the trenches, and poison-gas attacks than face the devil again.

The mother looked worried but the father had trouble suppressing a smile as the visitor earnestly and haltingly, for English was not his first language, unburdened himself of his angst. The boy, on the other hand, was shaken, although he did his best to hide his disquiet. Indian relatives had told him that for centuries native fishermen had left offerings of tobacco at a sacred rock that bore an uncanny resemblance to the head of an Indian chief on an island in Lake Muskoka, the largest of the lakes in the district, to appease spirits that inhabited the waters. He knew that his Indian grandfather would not think of fishing without first propitiating the god of the lake. Another relative now deceased was reputed to have had the ability to turn himself into a Bearwalker, a feared supernatural being in traditional native religion. His own mother had told him that a guardian spirit, from a dear uncle on the reserve who had died shortly before he was born, was watching out for him from beyond the grave. The story of the trapper seemed to be a confirmation that an invisible world existed in which good and evil spirits struggled to influence the destiny of the living.

Listening to the solemn words of his mother's cousin, who was clearly in despair since he was certain a horrible fate awaited him after death, the boy's throat constricted involuntarily until he nearly choked, and his skin erupted in goosebumps. In his innermost being, in that part of the psyche where logic does not penetrate, he believed the story of his mother's cousin unconditionally and was afraid the devil would find some reason to come looking for his soul as well. After the guest had departed, however, and as his mother looked on with quiet disapproval, the boy joined his father in laughing at the trapper. What superstition! How could any modern person believe such nonsense!

Listening from the safety of his bed to the moaning coming from outside, however, the boy regretted making fun of the trapper and came to the conclusion that what he was really hearing were cries of pain as the devil tormented the soul of the suicide victim. Then, paying closer attention, he believed he could make out other voices in the wind – native voices.

His mother had told him that long before the arrival of the white man, and not far from where their house was located, native people had built on the Indian River – just below the rapids that they called Baisong, or Thunder – a thriving community they named Obajewanung, or Gathering Place, complete with comfortable log cabins and fields of potatoes and corn. When missionaries had pushed into their territory and tried to convert them, they had rebuffed their efforts and remained faithful to their traditional native spirituality and practices. Their success had been their undoing. When the district was opened for settlement late in the nineteenth century, the government of the day, on the lookout for good places to locate settlers, lost no time in sending surveyors to Obajewanung to carve their lands into lots and to order the people to vacate their homes and leave.

The Indians made a desperate appeal to be allowed to remain in their ancestral homes but to no avail. Not having embraced Christianity, they received no support from the churches. In short order they were moved against their will to a rocky, inhospitable island in the Georgian Bay, where they were forced to return to the hand-to-mouth existence of their forebears, living in tents and relying on hunting and fishing rather than on agriculture for survival. The settlers then moved in and occupied their homes and fields. The graves of their ancestors were ploughed over, the names Baisong and Obajewanung were forgotten, and the long narrative of what had recently been the most important First Nation community in Muskoka was ignored when the history of early settlement in the district was compiled.

Tossing and turning, the thought came to the boy that the souls of these long-dead people might have returned from the Indian spirit world and now were pleading with him, as someone with roots in both the native world and that of the settlers, to become their champion when he became a man and to rectify the injustices done to them so many years ago. That did not reassure him. He was as much afraid of wandering souls with noble causes as he was of tormented ghosts and the devil.

The boy tried to push his fears to one side and deal with the issues logically, just as his father would. He wondered if more Indians than whites believed in ghosts, lost souls, spirits, and the devil. If the answer was yes, and he believed in them as well, did that mean he was more Indian than white? Would his father be disappointed in him if that turned out to be the case? Would he call him a "superstitious Indian"?

On the other hand, would his mother be upset if he took the side of his father? Would she think that he was betraying his native roots? She had, after all, been hurt when he had laughed at her cousin's belief. It was all very confusing, and he did not want to choose between his parents. More than anything else, however, he passionately needed to free himself from his crippling fear of ghosts, spirits, and the devil. Fighting instinct with logic, he told himself fiercely that they simply did not exist. He hoped that his mother and her people would understand.

The sounds of the moaning in the trees and the voices in the wind came to an end.

TWO

—

The Call

THEN THE BOY'S GREAT-GRANDFATHER came to visit. He was a long-retired preacher of a small fundamentalist denomination, highly regarded within his church, who despite his great age was still on the road spreading the gospel. The son of a well-off farmer in Southern Ontario, he had abandoned farm and inheritance more than seventy years earlier, when Ontario was still in the horse-and-buggy era, after receiving a call from God to carry the word of the Lord to the people. His photograph, an ancient daguerreotype taken some time in the latter part of the previous century, adorned one of the walls of the family's downstairs living quarters. It revealed a handsome young man with prematurely greying hair striking a heroic

Napoleonic pose, one hand inside his jacket on his chest and the other holding a Bible.

But while the other members of the family held their distinguished relative in awe, the boy's father had no use for him. After a few glasses of raisin wine, he could be induced to recount in detail, and with ever greater exaggeration with each retelling, an incident from his early childhood that had marked him for life. The clergyman had visited his family home, and as was the custom in his devout Christian family, everyone knelt down to pray. The old gentleman, however, had a phenomenal memory and was able to quote the Bible at extraordinary length, a feat that earned him the admiration of the faithful, but which led to inordinately long prayers.

The boy's father, then only five, fell asleep during one such session. This provoked the wrath of the preacher whose moral code was based on the harsh strictures of the Old Testament and who believed in using strong measures to discipline the young. With a leather razor strop he grimly whipped the bare bum of the child who, as he grew up, neither forgot nor forgave. The boy's father told his children that he became an atheist at that moment. Although he always laughed when he told this story, he was not joking. The boy, for his part, was secretly happy that the lashing his father had received had turned him into an opponent of corporal punishment where his own children were concerned.

The boy's mother broke the news of the impending visit to his father late one evening when she thought all the children were asleep. The boy listened intently, having no trouble hearing their whispering voices through the thin walls. His mother told her husband she had received a letter from the old clergyman announcing his wish to use the family home as a base to preach to the fifty to sixty Indians who were spending the summer as usual at the Indian Camp. Even before his father spoke, the boy knew what his response would be.

"No! No! And no! I don't want that old hypocrite in our house!"

His mother, on the other hand, was a peacemaker. Forced to make compromises all her married life to fit into the white man's world, it was second nature for her to try to persuade her husband to welcome the visitor.

"But, he's your own grandfather. We can't turn him away."

Listening to their heated discussion, the boy knew how it would end. His mother would get her way by ignoring his father and doing what she thought best. His father would grumble but do nothing to stop her, aware that her judgment was usually better than his. He would also devise a plan to deal with his unwelcome relative in his own way.

The boy was happy. He looked forward to meeting his father's grandfather, and knew he ran no risk of receiving the same sort of punishment his father had suffered so many years before. The old man was now more than ninety and would not be able to catch him if he tried. He was also confident his mother would protect him should he transgress his great-grandfather's rules. Just to be on the safe side, however, he decided to make a determined effort to stay awake during prayers, whatever their duration.

Late one Sunday afternoon, the mother and her two boys waited expectantly outside the village post office where the local bus delivered and collected its daily load of passengers. The boy and his brother ran to greet the white-haired old gentleman wearing a parson's collar who slowly descended the steps of the coach. The young clergyman in the photograph was gone and in his place was a patriarch with snow-white hair and gentle deep blue eyes. He smiled benignly at his half-breed great-grandchildren, asking them their names and shaking hands gravely with the mother. The boys then led him back to their home, all the while fighting for the honour of carrying his battered black suitcase.

From his observation post on the front porch, the father saw them coming. Not wanting to greet and make small talk with his grandfather, he slipped out the back door before they arrived, making for the bush behind the privy. There, a group of local reprobates joined him for a good, old-fashioned Muskoka raisin wine party, which had been timed to coincide with the arrival of his unwanted guest.

Of course, not just anyone was invited to the father's fête. Or perhaps it would be more accurate to say that not everyone would have come if invited. For in addition to being hierarchically separated into social classes based on wealth, with the merchants on top, the labourers below, and skilled workers in between, the villagers were unofficially divided into castes based on their drinking habits. The castes were three in number: the virtuous, the elite minority on top; the respectable, the great majority in the middle; and the reprobates, those left over at the bottom. But in contrast to the United Kingdom, the model for Canada's class system, and India, where the caste way of life originated, in democratic Canada people could move easily between classes and castes. All one had to do was to become more or less well off, or more or less virtuous, or more or less respectable. Many labourers occupied the exalted position of the virtuous. Many merchants were reprobates.

This informal caste system, which no one talked about but which existed in one form or another throughout the Ontario of the day, had emerged some years earlier as a result of the public passions and divisions over the morality of drinking. People clung to their divergent beliefs on booze with the same passionate intensity that they display today in the cultural wars between pro- and anti-abortion rights advocates and supporters of gay marriage and their opponents. Provincial governments were afraid to touch the subject and left it up to municipalities to decide for themselves whether they would be "wet" or "dry," by means of local-option plebiscites.

The villages and towns surrounding Port Carling were wet. Port Carling was dry. Within the village limits, there were no bars, taverns, or restaurants that served alcoholic drinks and no government outlets that sold bottles of beer and spirits. Many of the citizens took great pride in this state of affairs, believing it was a reflection of their intrinsic moral superiority over the degenerates elsewhere in the district.

Naturally, like Canadians everywhere, most villagers drank, even if they differed among themselves on the where, how, and what of consumption. The virtuous and the respectable bought their beer and spirits in far-off towns where they were not known and then sipped their drinks in solitude behind closed curtains in their homes or in the backrooms of their business establishments. They disagreed in one major area of drinking doctrine only. The virtuous, afraid they might be seen by their neighbours, never visited the nearby wet communities to imbibe in their beer parlours. The respectable, however, were prepared to take a chance. And if they had too much to drink and made fools of themselves, as occasionally happened, they would comfort themselves in their hangover remorse with the thought that at least they had sullied the purity of someone else's community rather than their own.

The virtuous and the respectable liked to think that they shared similar views on drinking issues, even if at times the virtuous had their doubts about the respectable. Both looked down on the reprobates, disdained imported store-bought wine as the beverage of foreigners, regarded Canadian vintages as the last resort of scoundrels and skid-row bums, and would not be caught dead drinking homebrew. Little old ladies from these worlds, it was true, occasionally broke the rules by quietly preparing batches of dandelion wine, but they drank it, they said, only for medicinal purposes.

Members of these castes never, ever put their empty booze bottles out with their trash to be picked up by the garbage collectors – who considered it part of their civic duty to let everyone know who was drinking what, when, and how much. Instead, late at night, after checking to be sure the coast was clear, they carefully inserted their empties in the garbage cans of their neighbours. In a pinch, members of both castes might turn to the village bootlegger for clandestine supplies of beer and spirits. Being from the virtuous caste himself, he understood their need for utter discretion, and quietly made home deliveries.

The reprobates, a minority in the village, did not care what gossip was being spread about them by the garbage collectors, proudly put their empties out in their own trash, frequented the beer parlours in neighbouring communities, did not worry if they acted silly after drinking too much, shamelessly consumed wine as well as beer and spirits in their homes, tried their hands at brewing up raisin wine from time to time, called their virtuous and respectable neighbours hypocrites, and agitated loudly and without success for the repeal of the regulations that kept Port Carling dry. They likewise were good customers of the bootlegger.

As for the native people, no one cared about their opinion. In class terms, they were invisible since they were so poor. As to caste, they would have been the untouchables had they lived in India. With few rights – they were not allowed to vote in provincial or federal elections and were barred by law from purchasing or possessing any sort of alcohol – they actually occupied neither class nor caste. They were forced to make raisin wine or to turn to the bootlegger for beer and liquor and to pay exorbitant prices for his illicit supplies.

The boy's father was a natural member of the reprobate caste. He had strong opinions on everything and loved poking fun at twaddle. He had no car to permit him to visit beer parlours in wet communities. And he did not have the money to buy from the bootlegger. He thus made raisin wine and held parties attended by other reprobates and his native friends.

They all came very willingly to the *soirée* he organized on the occasion of his grandfather's visit. Everyone had a great time guzzling homebrew, eating pickled eggs and mouth-burning salami sausages, and vying with each other in telling bawdy jokes and funny stories late into the night. The father was a natural storyteller and he kept his guests laughing with his embellished accounts of his days as a hobo and of his conversion to atheism. He also kept them amused by drawing on his stock of stories about Stephen Leacock, Canada's best-known humorous writer in the first half of the twentieth century. His knowledge was first-hand – his mother had once worked for the famous writer as a cook, and his sisters had been maids at the Orillia summer home of the author during the Great Depression. Leacock had even saved him from drowning – or claimed to have done so. The boy's father's irreverent description of the farcical rescue effort – involving an old launch, a seasick passenger, and a resourceful handyman – was the hit of the party.

Someone brought a guitar. Through his bedroom window, the boy listened to the festivities, enjoying in particular the maudlin renditions of their favourite tunes, especially the old nineteenth-century American ballad of the working man – "Frankie and Johnny" – the unofficial theme song of the reprobates.

Frankie and Johnny were Lovers.
O my gawd, how they could love,
They swore t'be true to each other
Just as true as the stars up above,
He was her man, but he done her wrong.

As raw alcohol, yeast, brine, hard-boiled eggs, hot peppers, indifferent meat, and garlic came together in the stomachs of the revellers, a nauseous mixture of unmentionable gases erupted in sulphurous blasts from both ends of the digestive tracts of host and guests alike in a storm of belching and passing of air that added immeasurably to the general hilarity.

As dawn approached, the guests drifted away to face the wrath of their wives for drinking too much, staying out so late, and returning home smelling as if they had spent the night sleeping in a pigsty. The father wove his way unsteadily down the footpath past the privy to the darkened house, highly satisfied with himself for having behaved so badly on the first night of his grandfather's visit. He hoped the racket made by him and his friends had kept the old man awake. Perhaps his grandfather would be so scandalized he would leave the village on the first bus out in the morning. Pushing open the screen door, a happy, tipsy grin on his face, he was looking forward to a good sleep for what remained of the night in his own bed.

His wife, however, waiting in the dark, had bad news.

"I have given your grandfather our bed and the old couch is mine. You can sleep on the floor. By the way, the old man is stone-deaf. He took his hearing aid out when he went to bed and didn't hear any of the shouting and carryings-on of your band of drunken louts."

Dejected, the father staggered outside looking for somewhere else to sleep, eventually crawling into a small hutch he had helped the boy construct for his pet rabbits. In the morning, when the boy went to feed them, he found the door open and his father stretched out on his back on the straw bedding sound asleep and smiling – with a rabbit on his chest.

The boy shook him awake. His father stared at him with bleary eyes until the world came into focus. Then he found out that it was harder to exit a low-ceilinged rabbit hutch sober than to enter one after having had too much to drink. After much muttering and writhing in the confined space, pushing with his elbows, pulling with his hands, and twisting with his torso, he eventually extracted himself from his prison and rolled out onto the tall dew-covered grass and weeds. He then scrambled to his feet, and without a word to his son, set off hurriedly for the back door of the house, anxious to leave for work on time.

The preacher grandfather may have had his moral code, but his nonconformist and raisin wine–drinking grandson had one of his own. The boy knew it well: never discipline children with razor strops, belts, or the back of one's hand; be kind to animals; and always report to work on time. Of the three, the third was the one that he repeated most frequently to his sons, whom he expected to follow in his footsteps one day as labourers.

"When you grow up and start work, my boys, remember these words of wisdom from your old dad: drink as much as you want at night, but never stay home from work the next day to sleep off your binges."

It was a matter of the highest principle, therefore, for the father to report to work and to be on time, no matter how awful he felt. Struggling down the path and into the house, he removed his shirt, dragged his body to the sink, turned on the tap, and took enormous swallows of ice-cold water to quell his hangover thirst. He then pushed his head under the flow, re-emerged, gasped for air, and noisily washed his face and chest. As he picked up a towel to dry himself, his eyes met those of his grandfather, who was sitting at the kitchen table. Neither spoke. The old man's face registered sadness, disappointment, and resignation.

The boy's mother, for whom respect for elders was central to her aboriginal culture and who genuinely liked her husband's grandfather, went out of her way to compensate for the boorish behaviour of her husband and to make the old man welcome. She cooked his meals, pressed his black clergyman's suit, washed his white shirts, and served him frequent cups of hot water – tea and coffee being forbidden in his religion. She also made arrangements with her relatives for him to preach at the Indian Camp and encouraged her children to attend the open-air services under the giant white pines along the Indian River bordering the reserve.

The boy, who did not know what to expect but who was caught up in the excitement of the preparations, could hardly wait to hear his great-grandfather speak. The first evening, freshly scrubbed in honour of the occasion, he ran down the narrow pathway leading from the business section of the village to the Indian Camp to secure for himself a choice place. The people turned out en masse, dressed in their best clothes.

Those who had them occupied aluminium lawn chairs; those who did not sat on wooden boxes. The boy joined a group of his friends sitting on the ground in front of the makeshift pulpit, nonchalantly mentioning that he just happened to be related to the preacher.

His great-grandfather, accompanied by his mother, then emerged from the cabin of a relative. His mother stood quietly at the rear of the crowd as the old patriarch walked slowly to the front, a smile on his face and his Bible in his hand. He was in his element, having addressed thousands of similar gatherings in his time. The native people, who likewise had attended numerous revivalist and camp meetings on their home reserves, knew what to expect.

The patriarch did not disappoint them. Punching the air with his fist, he called upon sinners to repent and passionately described how as a young man he had become a Christian through a life-altering and fervent religious experience. Those present, he said, could be saved as well, if only they would open up their hearts. There was much sympathetic nodding of heads, but no one took him up on his offer. Instead, someone asked whether she could lead the people in the singing of gospel hymns in Chippewa. He, of course, had no objection, and the crowd who knew the words of most Christian hymns by heart, sang song after song late into the night in the soft language of their ancestors, ending with the beautiful "Abide with me, Fast Falls the Eventide," sung first in Chippewa and then in English as a courtesy to the old preacher.

Pe we je we shin Ta ba ne ga yun,
Ah zhe mah ke pung ge she mo ke zis;
Ne je ke wa yug ne nuh guh ne goog,
Keen dush ween ka go nuh guh ne she kan.

Abide with me: fast falls the eventide,
The darkness deepens; Lord with me abide;
When other helpers fail, and comforts flee,
Help of the helpless, O abide with me.

So it was that for a week the people gathered to listen to the boy's great-grandfather and to sing hymns. The youngster was transfixed by the dramatic scenes, certain that he would never forget them no matter how long he lived, and he basked in the reflected esteem the Indians accorded to his great-grandfather. Even the boy's father, who as a matter of principle refused to attend the services, was attracted by the festive atmosphere and each night hovered in the background, trying to engage his friends in gossip.

Then, just before he left the village, the old clergyman called the boy to him, asked him to kneel, blessed him, and told him that he was destined to replace him one day as a preacher.

The prediction touched off great anxiety in the boy, for his great-grandfather, as he had frequently told the people in his sermons at the Indian Camp, had been converted in a traumatic scene, like Paul on the road to Damascus. Would the same thing happen to him? If so, when would the call come? How could a mere boy cope with the profundity and awesome power of the Lord? How could anyone, let alone a child, bear to face the creator one-on-one? Worst of all, the boy suspected that he had too many personal failings to be a preacher. He was not even certain what it meant to be a Christian, and was even less sure that he was one.

Night after night, the boy wrestled with these questions against the background sound of the now soulless, lonely, and impersonal wind outside his bedroom window. One night, he awoke, paralyzed by dread and consumed with fear. The silence was somehow deafening and the bedroom was filled with light that was blinding and incandescent. The boy told himself he was dreaming and that there was no logical explanation for what he was experiencing. He knew, however, that he was in the presence of the divine and was being asked to believe, to declare himself and to follow in the footsteps of his great-grandfather.

Too terrified to decide, the youngster made no commitment. After what seemed like an eternity, the light slowly faded. The boy, unable to accept his destiny, was left with an overwhelming feeling of spiritual failure, emptiness, and disappointment.

Shortly thereafter, he started attending Sunday school – an unlikely development given his father's views on religion. But his father worked hard six days a week, ten hours a day. With a pick and shovel he dug ditches, smashed stones with a sledgehammer, and drilled holes in rock for dynamite charges with a gang of men replacing rusted and damaged pipes in the village's antiquated water-distribution system. His only days off were Sundays, which were also when his wife's Indian relatives came to visit. Anxious to be rid of his squabbling children, if only for an hour or two while he held court at home, the father packed the lot of them, with the exception of the baby, off to the local church, accepting the risk that in the process they might become contaminated by religion.

Not having gone to church before, the boy paid close attention to the Sunday-school teacher when she talked about faith, saying one either had it or not. Only those with faith would go to heaven. The boy desperately wanted to go to heaven when he died and, if at all possible, to fulfill his great-grandfather's prophecy about his own future as a preacher. He prayed fervently for a miracle but did so without hope, aware that he had already had his chance, receiving but resisting the call.

The more he prayed, the more he thought of his denials of the nighttime moanings around the apple tree, of the devil his mother's cousin had seen, and of the voices in the wind asking him to be a leader for the native people when he became a man. Reluctantly, the boy asked himself how he could accept the existence of the supernatural when applied to Christianity but not when it came to ghosts, the devil, and dispossessed spirits. He found no answer, however, and was devastated.

THREE

—

Tough Times

THE FOLLOWING YEAR, TOUGH economic times returned to the village. Victoria Day, the holiday celebrating the birthday of the Queen whose reign had spanned most of the nineteenth century, was the traditional occasion for summer residents to travel up from Toronto and the other big cities of the south to open their cottages and to put their boats in the water. In 1948, however, the village was unusually quiet on this day so important to the small tourist communities in cottage country across Canada. The old men gossiping as usual on the benches around the public docks predicted the season would be bad.

And it was. In normal years, the village was booming by Dominion Day on July 1, Canada's national holiday. Les Whyte the butcher, Mel Wallace the barber, John

Dixon the hardware dealer, Fred Hanna and Arnold Stephens the grocers, Mildred Wright the importer of fine cashmere sweaters, Bill Croucher the garage owner, as well as other merchants, ice-cream vendors, fishing-tackle suppliers, bait dealers, boat builders, canoe and rowboat rental operators, restaurant proprietors, and real estate agents usually found it hard to keep up with the demand. In fact, some of them, a minority to be sure, confident that there was more than enough business to go around, usually treated their clientele from the big cities with haughty rural superiority, making it clear they were doing them a favour when they served them.

But such was not the case that fateful summer. Tourist-lodge owners complained that business had not been so slow since the Great Depression. Plumbers, electricians, and carpenters grumbled that cottagers who the year before had undertaken to give them contracts renovating their premises had simply broken their promises. The steamboats that picked up hundreds of day trippers from Toronto each morning at the railway terminus at the southern end of Lake Muskoka were bringing only half their normal complement of passengers to shop in the village. To make matters worse, the company that ran the daily bus service from the nearby town a half-hour away went bankrupt. When the village council decided to suspend funding for repairs on the municipal waterworks, the gang of labourers could not be paid, and the boy's father was laid off.

It was not the first time his father had lost his job. Happy-go-lucky by nature, he was not overly concerned. In the past, when work evaporated in one place, he had simply left his wife and children behind and gone off in search of employment wherever he could find it. Then, job in hand, he would send for his family, and life would continue as before. The pattern had been set in his years as a hobo during the Great Depression. Forgetting the hardships he had endured, he looked back with nostalgia on those times "on the bum," and never tired of recounting to his children his adventures riding the rails across the country and his encounters with tough railway cops, suspicious farmers, slovenly lumberjacks, hectoring schoolteachers, and revolutionary agitators. He had knocked on doors too numerous to remember, to beg for food in exchange for doing chores, visited more monasteries and churches in search of handouts than he could count, and had regularly been put up for the night in jail cells by good-hearted policemen when it was too cold to sleep outside.

After his marriage, he maintained a similar sort of itinerant life, moving from town to town in search of work, wife and growing family in tow. His boast was that he had always paid his bills, always provided food and shelter to his family, and had never, ever stooped to seek welfare. He had been in Port Carling for two years, he said, and it was time to move on.

"Let's sell the old house for whatever it will bring and use the money to get out of town. I've got itchy feet."

This time his wife said no.

"It's easy for you to say. I'm the one who always has to find a place to live. We've lived in tents more times than I can count! Never again! The children are older and deserve better. For the first time we've a house we can call our own, all fixed up and comfortable. It'll soon be paid off. You can do what you want, but I'm not budging."

She was bluffing, of course, but truly did not want to return to a transient life. Some years earlier the government had started a modest family allowance subsidy program to help families provide for the basic needs of their children. She was paying the mortgage on the house with the monthly cheques from Ottawa, and had even found the means to have electricity installed. It would soon be hers, and she did not want to start over again in a new town.

Although no one asked his opinion, the boy was on the side of his mother. His first years in the village had been hard. He had been held back a year by a teacher who treated him as an uneducable aboriginal despite being more advanced academically than most of his peers. When he first attended school, the other kids had called him a half-breed. Most did so without malice, thinking the use of slurs was normal in describing people different from themselves.

In fact, the children of the village and their parents – and for that matter most white, English-speaking Protestants of Canada of the period – would have been surprised if anyone had told them their language or behaviour was in any way racist. For generations, teachers, church leaders, and editorial writers had been telling the public that racism was a bad thing, adding that fortunately Canada was largely free of it. They pointed to Harriet Beecher Stowe's *Uncle Tom's Cabin*, in which American slaves fled to freedom along the famous Underground Railroad to Canada, there to live happily ever after among an enlightened population. They repeated that Canada, unlike the United States, had not engaged in genocidal frontier wars with its native peoples. Their chests swelled with pride as they noted the leading role being taken at that time in the United Nations by Prime Minister William Lyon Mackenzie King, Secretary of State for External Affairs Louis St. Laurent, and Undersecretary of State Lester Pearson in the fight for a more just world order.

The boy was only vaguely aware of the moralistic

message the members of Canada's opinion-forming elite had been expressing over the years and the selective, self-satisfied way the public had been interpreting it. He had been told by his mother, however, that the family who had sold the old house to her had left the village some years earlier largely because they had been subject to discrimination by their neighbours for being black. He had heard his father say that Indian war veterans, including one relative of his mother who had lost his leg in fighting in Northwestern Europe, had been turned down for membership in the Royal Canadian Legion close to their distant reserve because they were Indian. His father had also told him that native people had gone overseas to fight for a liberty they did not have at home, not even being allowed the right to vote like other Canadians despite their sacrifices. He understood, from listening to the conversations of his parents around the dinner table, that the government had refused the entry to Canada of Jews arriving at its borders, sending them back to Hitler's death camps, and that Japanese Canadians had been herded into concentration camps for the duration of the war.

And from personal experience, he knew a few kids – thankfully only a handful – who periodically revealed themselves to be as racist in spirit as in word. Like rats crawling from a sewer and with faces made ugly by hate – and emboldened by the unofficial sanction of village custom – they would call the boy and his brother dirty half-breeds and their mother a dirty squaw. Just as hurtful, he had to listen to racist banter in the schoolyard and in the streets about lazy, uneducated, and inferior Indians, talk that he could not help but take personally.

The mother dismissed these attacks by telling her children that Port Carling was their hereditary home in a way it could never be for the other villagers whose ancestors came from other parts of the world. Indians had lived in the region for thousands of years before the arrival of the white man. Most villagers had no idea of the origins of their families beyond the generation that had come to Muskoka in the late nineteenth century. She, however, could trace her family tree back to a hereditary chief who had greeted the British soldiers and administrators who first ventured into the lands of what would become Central Ontario in the late eighteenth century after the Seven Years War between Great Britain and France ended in 1763. These roots – this relationship between her children and the land, rock, and water of Muskoka – was something no one would ever be able to take from them.

Besides, she said, anti-Indian sentiment seemed to run in families. The sons and daughters of people who had called her names when she was a child were carrying on the tradition by targeting her children. Fortunately, she said, attitudes towards Indians had improved over the years in the village. Some of the people who had once treated her badly were now her friends. The situation locally was no worse than in any other town she had lived in since her marriage.

With the passage of time, helped by his light-coloured skin and his growing success in the classroom, the boy was no longer called racist names, and was promoted to the next grade on his second try. The damage was done, however, and although he would develop a passionate attachment to the village, for the rest of his days he would always feel that to some extent he was an outsider. Nevertheless, he was determined to get on with life.

And the people of the village, for reasons he did not understand, began to treat him as one of their own. Eventually, when he came to know them better, he would find that many of them, so gruff and reserved in appearance, were actually warm-hearted and fair-minded. Several stopped him on the street, told him they had heard that he was doing well at school, and encouraged him to persevere. A businessman who had no sons of his own invited him to a father-and-son banquet at the Lions Club. Another, knowing that he attended Sunday school but unaware of his spiritual bewilderment, asked him to consider becoming a United Church minister when he grew up. Several of the big boys from the high school took him under their wing and allowed him to join in some of their rough-house games, in particular one called "Knights and Horses," where they put youngsters on their backs and smashed into each other with wild abandon, ignoring bloody noses and bruised faces until there was only one knight and horse left standing on the playground.

The boy did not want to move to another town and start the process of trying to fit in once again. He had also made a good friend whom he did not want to leave. The friend was short, dark-complexioned, good-natured, and the same age. The two had first met when the boy's family lived in the tent near the dump. Despite losing to him in a fierce schoolyard battle – the only fight the boy would fail to win in his years at the school – the two had taken to each other. They got into minor scrapes and adventures worthy of Mark Twain's *Tom Sawyer*.

Once, they found a water snake, as thick as a man's wrist and as long as an axe handle, and in an inexcusable fit of cruelty, beat it to death. They dangled it at eye level from a branch overhanging the shadowed sidewalk across the highway from the old house and lay in wait in an adjoining clump of lilac trees.

Their efforts were quickly rewarded. When villagers

out for their evening walks bumped their heads against the bloody snake, raw instinct overcame them. Their first reaction was always frozen disbelief. Their faces turned deathly white, their eyes registered dread, and their mouths opened wide in soundless screams. Then, as adrenaline kicked in and they fled the scene, their frozen vocal cords thawed, releasing pent-up shrieks of the purest, most unadulterated – and in the opinion of the boys – most satisfying terror. Normally fearless veterans and macho athletes produced the same panicky reactions as mild grandmothers pushing baby carriages.

Best of all, having fled the scene, no one dared to return to remove the snake. The youngsters chortling in the bushes were able to watch repeat performances for two evenings until a crow came one morning to eat it, spoiling their fun.

Together they hunted partridges, rabbits, and ducks, the boy using a .22 rifle given to him by an old native friend of his grandfather. Together they shot porcupines and dragged the carcasses to the Indian Camp to sell to the ladies who dyed the quills red, blue, and green and used them together with sweetgrass and beads to decorate their birchbark and buckskin handicraft. Together they fished for catfish and black bass on the Indian River from an old and leaky rowboat supplied by the same native friend of his grandfather.

Together they built a clubhouse under the porch of the boy's home and a fort in the bush that they stocked with treasures scavenged from the village dump. Together they went on fishing and camping trips to remote lakes around the Georgian Bay with his friend's father, a single parent who had been wounded in the war.

The boy loved these expeditions and returned home each time with fresh supplies of salacious stories to recount to his parents, to the great delight of his father, a connoisseur of the art.

Worn down by his wife's resistance, the father gave up on his plan to relocate his family. In the absence of any local bus service, he set out on foot to look for work, carrying only a change of clothes and his empty lunch box in a shopping bag. Eventually a passing motorist picked him up and dropped him in a larger town some distance away. The father had promised to send his wages to his wife as soon as he found a job. In the interim, the mother found herself in a desperate situation, with no money to feed her children, pay her water bills, and settle her tax accounts. Nervously she ran up a big bill at Hanna's General Store, hoping her good record in settling her accounts since she had arrived in the village would stand her in good stead. The kind-hearted Fred Hanna, who knew her father, obliged.

The town clerk did not, coming repeatedly to her door.

"Pay your water and tax bills right now or I'll cut off your water and sell your house for taxes."

The mother was frantic but could do nothing about it.

FOUR

—

The Mother

ON A WEDNESDAY MORNING IN early July, a telegram arrived from her uncle on the distant reserve:

> Your father dead. Wake tomorrow night. Funeral Friday. Come home.
> Uncle Jack

The news from her uncle was not unexpected. The mother's father had been in declining health for years. Like other Indians, he had lived a hard subsistence existence outside the mainstream of Canadian society with its ready access to medical care, decent food, and proper education. Like all native Canadians of the period, he lived and died as a non-person, not recognized as a full citizen under Canadian law. Never one to complain, he had accepted this way and rhythm of life.

As a young man, he had left the reserve looking for work. At first, he served as a guide and canoeist for survey parties mapping the boundary between Ontario and Manitoba. Later, he was a logger in bush camps, where he excelled in the amateur wrestling matches organized for the entertainment of the men during the long winter months. Then followed a stint during the Great War in an ammunition plant, during which he was so badly injured in an accident that he had to return to the reserve. There he married a woman much younger than himself who had just spent five years in a tuberculosis sanatorium.

The early years of their marriage were happy ones. His father-in-law, who had returned from the Great War with lungs ravaged by mustard gas during fighting on the Western Front, received a small pension from the Canadian government that he shared with his extended family. Each spring, the couple took the train to Lake Muskoka, where they had stored their canoe over the winter months. Then after an easy six-hour paddle, they reached the Indian Camp in Port Carling, to spend their summers with friends and family from the reserve. During one of these summers, the boy's mother was born.

Shortly thereafter the marriage fell apart. The wife, it turned out, loved drinking hard liquor, quarrelling and fighting with fist and foot. Her war-hero father then died after years of coughing up blood from his damaged lungs. With his death the disability pension payments stopped, eliminating the family's economic safety cushion. Frittering away her inheritance on drink, the mother saw her family go from one of the better off on the reserve to one of the poorest. Worse, she was cruel to her daughter, beating her mercilessly for the most minor faults, and keeping her out of school for lengthy periods.

When the couple broke up, they had five children, the youngest a boy of six months. The wife took one child with her, another was adopted by an aboriginal family on a nearby reserve, while the father inherited two boys, including the baby. The eldest daughter, who would become the boy's mother, soon got married, persuading a doubtful minister that she was eighteen rather than fourteen, her real age. In those days, Indian women who married non-Indians lost their legal status as Indians, their membership in the band, and their right to live on the reserve. The curse extended to their children, who likewise were denied Indian status. The new bride was thus forced out of her home community and did not have the right to spend her summers with her new husband at the Indian Camp in Port Carling.

She did not care, for life on the reserve had been harsh, and she wanted a better future for her children.

The Indian girl had joined the great army of Canada's working poor when she married the young white man. And for years to come, although not really on the margins of society, the mixed-race couple would be among the worst off economically. As children arrived, the growing number of mouths to feed left the Indian wife, now a mother, unable to afford to travel to visit her father on the reserve. She had rejoiced, therefore, in the summer of 1946 to see her father again at the Indian Camp after so many years apart, to speak to him at length in her native language, and to introduce him to her four children.

His once-great strength was a thing of the past, and his health was already failing. Each day, he would depart early in his canoe to fish for food – and to sell to the tourists and summer residents who came to his cabin each evening in search of fresh lake trout. The money he received he spent on flour, baking powder, and lard to make bannock, as well as on tea, sugar, and canned evaporated milk. Apart from the fish, the diet was unhealthy in the extreme, and his face and body were bloated and sallow.

The baby boy he had undertaken to raise when his wife left him a decade earlier was with him when the mother took her brood to meet their Indian grandfather. Now a ten-year-old with rotting teeth from eating raw sugar and candy, he found it amusing that his nephews were only a little younger than he was. The grandfather, for his part, greeted his grandchildren affectionately. The boy was enormously impressed with his quiet natural dignity and wisdom, and often went on his own to the Indian Camp that summer to sit quietly at his side and to soak up the atmosphere, his first exposure to the lifestyle and culture of his mother before she had entered the white man's world.

The grandfather was too sick to return to Port Carling the following year, and the boy's mother did not see her father again until the spring of 1948. At that time, a neighbour with a car who was travelling to a nearby town offered to make a detour to the reserve and let her call on her father. The boy and his brother accompanied their mother on their first visit to her childhood home. Her home reserve, the boy expected, would resemble the Indian Camp, where the people lived in neat cabins doubling as handicraft shops that smelled of sweet grass, of fresh birchbark and the wood of the ash tree pounded with the back of an axe into strips and used to make baskets. At the Indian Camp, footpaths ran from home to home and no roads disturbed the primeval scene. At the Indian Camp, pine needles carpeted the forest floor. At the Indian Camp, families sat in the evenings around their campfires, telling stories, frying fish, and roasting beaver or porcupines just as their ancestors had in centuries past. At the Indian Camp, canoes were pulled up along the shores of a magnificent bay. The setting could have been taken from a painting by the great nineteenth-century interpreter of native life, Paul Kane. In the boy's imagination, the same romantic scene would prevail at the mother's home reserve.

On the way to the grandfather's house, the boy's mother warned her sons not to be disappointed. The reserve, she emphasized, was not the Indian Camp; conditions there were difficult. Few people had jobs and most survived by whatever casual labour they could find on neighbouring farms and tourist resorts, by trapping on their traditional lands to the north in Muskoka, by fishing, trading for vegetables with local farmers, and by gathering and selling ginseng roots to Chinese Canadians. Others made baskets, axe handles, paddles, quill boxes, and junky artifacts such as toy birchbark canoes and small imitation wooden war hatchets to sell door-to-door locally in the winter and at their cabins at the Indian Camp and the cottages of summer residents on the Muskoka Lakes in the summer.

The most destitute received small handouts from the Indian agent. Backed by RCMP constables, he was responsible for enforcing the provisions of the hated Indian

Act. Like a district commissioner sent from London to govern the locals in a British colony in the old days of the empire, he was the paternal, all-powerful overlord who controlled all aspects of Indian life.

It had been different in the past, the boy's mother said. Hundreds of years before, the ancestors of the Chippewa, the Anishnaabeg people, had moved out of their homelands in the Canadian Shield, along the Georgian Bay and in the vast rocky, lake-studded forests of the northwest, to take over the fertile lands of Southern Ontario, homeland of the Iroquoian people but abandoned by them after vicious inter-tribal civil wars in the seventeenth century. Her family was part of a large band or community known as the Chippewas of Lake Huron and Lake Simcoe, who occupied the territory just to the south of Muskoka. They supplemented their traditional hunting and fishing way of life by adopting the slash-and-burn farming practices of the Iroquois they displaced, which allowed them to grow corn and squash. Together with other native peoples in what would eventually be called Canada, and alongside waves of Indian warriors from the Ohio Valley under Tecumseh, they fought on the side of the British in the War of 1812. The history books, she told her children, said native intervention at the start of the war had prevented the Americans from conquering the British colony. She was proud of the fact that her ancestors had fought in the conflict, some emerging as decorated war heroes.

Those had been glorious years. Not long after the end of the War of 1812, however, the government of the day removed her people from their farms and cabins to make way for settlers moving north in search of land. It divided the community into three groups, sending two to live on reserves established on isolated islands on Lake Simcoe and the Georgian Bay and the third to a new reserve created on a rocky, inhospitable tract of land abandoned by pioneers as unfit for cultivation. Her family, the mother said, was sent to the third reserve. The people counted themselves lucky. It was only through the intervention of the British government that plans by the colonial administration to round up and banish the Anishnaabeg people of Southern Ontario to a much more remote northern reserve were abandoned. Since that time, it was only when spending their summers at the Indian Camp, where the people could return to a semblance of their traditional life, that they came alive in spirit.

The boy's mother had been wise to warn her sons. As they passed the sign welcoming visitors to the reserve, the paved road turned into a dusty, potholed gravel track. Later, looking back as a well-travelled adult, he would remember it as Canada's Third World. Bloated bodies of dogs and cats, killed by speeding cars, lay uncollected in the ditches. People the boy had met at the Indian Camp and now recognized walking along the road seemed bereft of the self-confidence and dignity he had come to associate with them in their Muskoka setting. Yellow-stained mattresses, car bodies, old magazines, shattered bottles that once contained cheap wine, perfume, and patent medicines, chewing tobacco packages, cigarette butts and wrappings, and broken household equipment littered weed-filled yards. With some exceptions, the habitations were the dilapidated log cabins and tarpaper-roofed shacks of a rural slum. Few of the homes were connected to the electric grid that ran through the community, connecting the better-off white families on either side of the reserve, and outhouses were standard in all backyards. The home of his grandfather was no different from the others.

The neighbour from Port Carling dropped the mother and children off at the entrance to the lane, took one look at the grandfather's house, and sped away, saying she would be back to pick them up in thirty minutes. The mother's young brother, now twelve years old, his front teeth rotted away and the others black from decay, gave them an enthusiastic welcome. His face was grimy and his dirty bare feet could be seen beneath tattered trousers held up by a piece of string. The boy felt ashamed of himself for flinching when his young uncle gave him a hug. Visibly ailing and malnourished, the boy's grandfather struggled to his feet to greet his daughter, who could barely restrain her tears on seeing her father in such a state.

Her father had suffered a stroke and was blind. He was, however, in his own words "getting by." Each week, he sent his young son to the Indian agent who provided money for tea and canned evaporated milk as well as for lard, flour, and baking powder. The son prepared rudimentary meals for his father every day, and someone had strung a rope from the back exit of the house to the privy, allowing the old man to grope his way to the toilet.

It was a return to the unhappy past for the boy's mother, who could hardly wait to leave. She knew her father would not live long. Indeed, she wanted to take him and her young brother home with her. But that was out of the question. Her husband would be opposed, since he could barely feed his wife and children as it was. With six family members already stuffed into the three-room house, no space remained for anyone else. She shoved a handful of change, all the money she possessed, into his hands, called to her boys, and fled to the waiting car.

Now, just a few months later, the boy's Indian grandfather was dead. His mother felt guilty and emotionally crushed. Perhaps if she had simply taken her father to her home, she could have persuaded her husband to let her care for him. Perhaps he could have slept on the old couch. Perhaps old Fred Hanna would have given her credit at his store to feed him. Perhaps he would have received better medical care and lived longer in the white village of his daughter. To add to her torment, she was well aware that in accordance with aboriginal custom, everyone back home expected her, as the oldest child, even if she was no longer a member of the community, to attend the wake and funeral. But, she told herself, that was impossible. She did not have the money to pay the taxi and bus fares to reach the reserve, and could not in any case leave her children alone.

Guilt-stricken, unable to grieve properly, deeply worried at the growing debt at the grocery store, she was caught between two cultures. Pushed by the grim town clerk's relentless demands that she pay the water bill and taxes, and psychologically damaged by the life of hopelessness and deprivation she had endured as a child on the reserve, she fell into a deep depression. Scarcely able to walk or talk, she nevertheless forced herself day after day to take care of her children. At times, she would take her corncob pipe, tobacco and matches, and to the great distress of her sons, who feared she might come to harm, would vanish into the bush to smoke quietly by herself for hours on end in an effort to pull herself together. But to no avail. Seeking help, she visited the village doctor, promising to pay him for his services when she could. In this era before the invention of anti-depression medication, he could do little other than to offer her sympathy.

The boy's father then returned home for a weekend. He had found work as a railway section hand in the distant town, and he had triumphantly brought money to pay the tax and water bills and to settle the account at the grocery store. Shocked at the condition of his wife, however, he immediately quit his job to care for his children, and sent for his mother to help out. A deeply generous person and a pious daughter of the old clergyman who had visited Port Carling a year earlier, she was fond in her own way of her Indian daughter-in-law. When her son had come home with an aboriginal wife, she had scotched a revolt by her daughters, who resented the new arrival, by telling them that all people, Indians included, were equal in the eyes of God. Using her considerable authority, she had insisted that they treat their new sister-in-law with respect. She also liked her daughter-in-law's father, welcoming him to her house whenever he was in the neighbourhood. The same did not apply to his estranged wife. She sent her away and told her she was not welcome in her home when she once appeared on her doorstep.

The mother-in-law treated her son's young wife with great affection as a member of her own family, taught her to cook the food of the white man, how to raise children, and how to manage a household. Over the years, she had done what she could to help her son and his growing household financially, but her means were limited. Her own husband, a Scottish immigrant, toiled in low-paying factory jobs all his life and was frequently unemployed. When the children arrived, the new grandparents were proud and caring, and found ways to bring them to their rented home for extended stays in the summer and during the Christmas holidays. The old couple were even planning to move to Port Carling to be close to their grandchildren as soon as they were eligible to receive their old-age pensions.

The boy's grandmother was from the generation that had lived through epidemics of scarlet fever, diphtheria, typhoid fever, polio, smallpox, and the other diseases that struck fear into Canadians in the late nineteenth and early twentieth centuries. Her own mother was a victim of the influenza pandemic that broke out in the last days of the Great War. In her day, neighbours helped neighbours combat these illnesses, and she had been always among the first to arrive and the last to depart from the sickbed of those in need. Thus she responded with alacrity to the appeal when her son asked for her help. Quickly shopping for presents for her grandchildren, she packed a large suitcase, donned the clothes she wore to church, and set off at once for Port Carling.

His grandmother was already sitting on the old couch under her clergyman father's framed photograph when the boy returned home after running an errand in the village. Before he saw her, he heard her talking to his mother.

"Now you must pull yourself together! Your husband and children need you. The police will come for you and lock you up in the insane asylum if you don't straighten yourself out! Then who will cook for your husband and children?"

The boy walked in to join his brother and sisters, who were silently opening the presents brought by his grandmother. His mother sat quietly as her mother-in-law continued to tell her there was nothing wrong with her and that people in her condition simply spent too much time thinking about their own problems and not enough about the needs of others. Slowing down momentarily to give her grandson a hug and his present, the grandmother resumed her well-intentioned rebuke, thinking all her daughter-in-law needed was a good reprimand. Reflecting the attitudes of her generation, she had no sympathy whatsoever for anyone suffering from what she called "bad nerves." To her, "bad nerves" were a character defect that could only be overcome by positive thinking.

The boy's grandmother left soon afterwards, believing that her "pull yourself together" mission had been accomplished. Not knowing what to do or who to turn to, the boy's mother gathered her children together to tell them she was ill but that she still loved them. Give her time to get well, she asked. And they did.

FIVE

—

The Hero

THE BOY STARTED SCHOOL IN the fall in a rebellious mood, bitterly angry at the harsh treatment meted out to his mother by the village clerk and intensely worried by her deepening depression. He spoke to no one about his concerns and was, as usual, quiet and studious in the classroom. Outside, however, he escaped to an imaginary world, one shaped by comic books and newsreel stories of the recent war.

On one exploration mission to the dump, he found a discarded army helmet and a large box of pointed wafer cups for making ice cream cones that had been thrown out by a restaurant owner at the close of the tourist season. Placing the helmet on his head, he instantly became a Second World War Canadian commando. Lost in his new identity and with the helmet perched precariously on his head – for it was several sizes too large – he carried the box of cones to the road running through the village. Carefully checking that no one was watching, he arranged them just below the brow of a hill to look like giant spikes. He then slipped into the bush on the side of the road, found a good hiding place, and waited.

In his imagination, he was now behind Nazi lines, ordered to stop a convoy of German motorized troops en route to block the Allied invasion of Normandy. The other Canadian commandos on the mission had been killed in unbelievably violent fighting, and he was the only survivor. It was thus up to him, and to him alone, to accomplish the mission. After killing hundreds of enemy soldiers in fierce hand-to-hand fighting, he had managed to seize a huge supply of landmines from a German ammunition dump and had arranged them on the only road leading to the front.

Oblivious to the clouds of blackflies feasting on his flesh and disregarding the ants that crawled over him as he lay in his hideout, the boy's mind jumped ahead. In his fantasy world, the German transport trucks had come over the hill only to be blown to smithereens by the landmines. He had risen to his feet and was machine-gunning thousands of evil Nazi storm troopers.

He then saw himself standing at attention on the grounds of Buckingham Palace. He was wearing the helmet he had found at the dump and was in full-dress combat uniform. King George VI, smiling sadly – for he alone was aware of the hardships and suffering the boy had endured and the sacrifices he had made – was pinning the Victoria Cross on his chest. His parents, all the kids from the school, the teachers, and everyone else from the village, as well as British prime minister Winston Churchill and Canadian prime minister William Lyon Mackenzie King were present. The crowd was cheering and ever so proud of the exploits of the humble boy from Port Carling.

"I thank you on behalf of the Royal Family, the British Empire, the citizens of Canada, and the people of the village of Port Carling for single-handedly and against all odds saving the entire Allied Expeditionary Force, pinned down on the beaches in Normandy and about to be thrown into the sea in the face of fierce German attacks."

Screeching tires brought the boy back to reality. A local real estate agent, blind in one eye, had come over the crest of the hill. He slammed on the brakes and twisted the steering wheel in a frantic attempt to avoid what he thought were genuine upturned spikes – and skidded into the ditch. Fortunately, he had been driving slowly and was not injured.

His daydream interrupted, the boy removed his helmet and slipped away through the bush to his home, thinking it best not to tell anyone of his afternoon exploits.

Some time later, the boy was moseying along back to school after lunch, lost in thought as always. He put his hand in his pocket, touched some nails, and had a Proustian moment. The youngster had never heard of Marcel Proust, author of one of the greatest French novels *Remembrance of Things Past*. If he had, he would have known that at the turn of the century in his Parisian apartment, Proust once dipped a special type of French sweet biscuit called a *madeleine* into a cup of tea, raised it to his mouth, and nibbled on it delicately. This one fleeting encounter between tea-soaked French cookie and sensitive palate stirred in him a veritable flood of memories and associations that the great French aesthete put down on paper, and in doing so influenced the course of literature.

Something similar happened to the boy. As in the case of Proust, physical contact led to the arousal of memories. They would not lead to greatness, however, and would set off a train of events that could have had dire consequences for him. For the encounter of sweaty fingers with sharp, pointed galvanized nails reminded him of the fun he and his best friend had had the previous weekend when they hauled abandoned wooden orange crates, old cardboard boxes, cast-off pieces of plywood, and discarded planks from the dump to fix up their fort hidden in the bush. They had brought hammers and nails, several of which the boy had forgotten in his pocket, and together they had made their redoubt impregnable against hostile attack.

He then noticed he was passing in front of Arnold Stephen's grocery store, located halfway up a steep hill. A truck was parked in front, its motor was running, and its back door lay open, revealing cases of soup, vegetables, breakfast cereal, oranges, apples, and the usual array of grocery products. The driver was not to be seen and the boy assumed that he was inside talking to the easygoing storekeeper.

Suddenly the youngster was in Nazi-occupied Norway in 1942. He was the only Canadian member of a team of skilled saboteurs landed by a British submarine at a deserted fjord. Its mission was the destruction of a supply of heavy water, the secret component needed by Germany to make the atomic bomb. The Norwegian underground had sent an urgent and secret message to London warning that a truck loaded with the deadly material was scheduled to leave for Berlin at any moment. If the consignment got through, Germany would win the war.

The Norwegians met the Allied team as it came ashore in its rubber dinghy and took it to their fort hidden in the bush. The Nazis, however, tipped off by a spy, attacked and destroyed their stronghold. It had recently been reinforced with the highest quality orange crates, cardboard boxes, and planks, but the Germans managed to smash their way through the defences. Everyone, with the exception of the brave Canadian, was killed. But against all odds, he fought his way out of the fort, killing hundreds if not thousands of Germans in the process. And after incredible adventures, he made his way to the hidden place where the truck loaded with the heavy water was parked.

It just so happened that it was parked on the side of a hill, its motor running, its open back door revealing cases of the dreaded heavy water. The driver was nowhere to be seen. The Canadian hero had to act quickly or else Hitler would win the war! He knew what to do! He would sabotage the tires!

The boy looked around to see if there were any Nazi sentries watching. There were none. He knelt down, took the nails from his pocket, and laid them upright between the road and the tires in such a way that they would penetrate the rubber as soon as the truck started to move.

"Take that, evil Nazis!"

Running up the hill towards the school, he had second thoughts. What had he done? There were no trucks filled with heavy water in Port Carling! What if someone had seen him? The driver would be really mad! And a truck tire probably cost a fortune! If he were caught, he would be sent to the notorious reformatory for boys at Bowmanville!

Rushing back, he arrived to see the driver slam shut the rear door of his truck, wave to his friend the storekeeper, and move towards his cab. Too late! The boy returned to school. There were no repercussions. No one had seen him, and when the tires went flat, the truck driver probably assumed he had run over the nails on the road.

There was worse to come. The village council authorized a resumption of the waterworks project and the boy's father, a favourite of the foreman, was offered his old job back. This time, however, he was given the added responsibility of setting dynamite charges as the crew worked its way through the rocky terrain. The father was delighted. He already fancied himself to be a connoisseur on the making and drinking of homemade raisin wine. Now he would be able to show his friends he was a specialist in dynamite as well. He had, in fact, once worked in a gold mine and had watched as real experts supervised the drilling of rock, the insertion of nitroglycerine caps into sticks of dynamite, the careful attachment of wires to the caps, the fastening of the wires to a battery, and finally the touching of the wires together to create a spark that set off the explosions.

The father's theoretical knowledge was sound, but he was not experienced in the practical application of the art of blasting. It took him some time to learn how to judge exactly how much dynamite was needed for each job, and until he developed a feel for his new calling, he erred in the direction of using too much rather than too little high explosive. Not that anyone on the waterworks gang minded. The big explosions, the shattering of windows, and the dramatic scattering of boulders and shattered rock throughout the village enlivened their otherwise tedious days.

The boy's father probably could have found a better place to keep his supply of dynamite and nitroglycerine caps than under the stairs leading up to the bedrooms. But he had already persuaded his wife to let him store in this handy location two gallons of raisin wine left over after his summer of drinking outside behind the privy. It just made sense to him to store explosives and wine together, since they were the raw materials of his show-and-tell sessions.

When visitors arrived, he would crawl under the stairs and emerge with a gallon of the light-brown liquid that looked more like swamp water than wine. After depositing the jug on the kitchen table, he would fetch the requisite number of water-glasses from the cupboard, fill them with homebrew, and add to each what he claimed was his secret ingredient. Picking up a glass, he would raise it to his nose, pretend to sniff its bouquet like a sommelier in one of the select restaurants he been thrown out of in his hobo days, and hold it in the air to let everyone admire its superior body. He would then sip it loudly, roll it around in his mouth, smack his lips with exaggerated satisfaction, and pronounce it the equal of the finest champagnes.

With his trademark good-natured and cackling laugh, he would tell his guests that the secret ingredient was simple food colouring.

"If you change the colour of even the poorest of wines," he would say, "you will change attitudes towards it."

His favourite colour was purple since it was the colour of kings, and it made his wine look like high-class French hooch.

His guests always smiled appreciatively, but they could not have cared less about the colour. They would humour him by requesting green, black, or yellow servings, but they really looked forward only to the high they got from its deadly alcohol content.

After serving generous glasses of wine, coloured to taste, the father would revisit his store of treasures under the stairs and return with a half-dozen sticks of dynamite in one hand and four or five nitroglycerine caps in the other. It was showtime. Waving dynamite and caps in the air, he would describe how much explosive power there was in just one stick of cordite. He would then add other relevant details designed to impress the credulous. Once he even opened the lid of the woodstove, and with great theatrical flair, threw a stick of dynamite into the fire. He laughed heartily as everyone ran for cover.

Dynamite without a cap, he claimed, was inert. Only when shocked by the explosion of a nitroglycerine cap, itself sparked by a surge of electricity, would it explode. The caps were another story. They were volatile and powerful. A single cap improperly handled, he said, was capable of blowing off a hand or foot. Sometimes it just took the body heat of a workman's hand to set off a particularly unstable one.

The boy listened with particular attention as his father explained to his friends the qualities of nitroglycerine caps. He hoped there were no unstable caps in the pile tossed together in a bag and stowed alongside five or six cases of dynamite under the stairs. An explosion would obliterate the family home, and probably the outhouse as well, in one huge blast of powder and wine. But his father, he assumed, had already thought of that.

The boy had other concerns. The Nazi enemy, he

knew, was lurking at the dump, just waiting for the chance to seize the village. But now he had the perfect weapon to deal it such a blow it would never threaten anyone again!

After quietly taking a fistful of caps from the store under the stairs, he linked up with his best friend, who also understood the need to strike the enemy before it attacked the unsuspecting village. His friend dug his father's army helmet out of the duffle bag of souvenirs he had brought back from the war. The boy equipped himself with the helmet he had found some time earlier, and together the two set off just before dark up the gravel road leading to the dump. The enemy, they had reason to believe, came out to eat at this time of day.

To maintain the element of surprise, they left the road well before they reached the site of the dump. Pushing through a wall of dust-covered thistles and burdocks that flourished in the sunlight on the side of the road, they checked that they were not being followed, and carefully made their way by a circuitous route through thorny tangles of raspberry and blackberry bushes and dense underbrush to a low hill overlooking the enemy camp. They then crawled as quietly as they could on their hands and knees to within attacking distance of the foe hidden in a load of food scraps that had been dropped off some time earlier by a truck from a tourist hotel.

They heard the rustling of feet. Peering out from under their oversized helmets, they soon spotted the enemy itself. So the intelligence they had received from military headquarters was right! The enemy was present in strength and was eating its dinner!

The uninformed might have thought that they were hearing and seeing common grey rats devouring kitchen slop. The boys, however, were not fooled. The evil Nazis, everyone knew, were masters of disguise!

Then with mighty cries befitting their role as fierce, highly trained Canadian commandos, and with their helmets bouncing on their heads, the boys leapt to their feet and rushed the stinking pile of garbage, hurling the caps transformed into hand grenades at the enemy. On striking the refuse, they exploded with huge blasts, momentarily startling the brave soldiers but lifting potato peels, carrot scrapings, apple cores, corn husks, banana skins, coffee grounds, well-chewed steak bones, chicken entrails, and other delicacies – along with rats, of course – high into the air.

This was even better than the boys had expected! They quickly cast their reserve grenades at the survivors, who were scurrying for cover like the cowards they were. And, mission accomplished, the boys returned to base, tired but ready to fight another day.

SIX

—

Trick or Treat

THEN SOMETHING HAPPENED THAT almost cured the boy of his obsessive daydreaming. One morning he left for school in a particularly pensive mood, for he had dreamed the night before that he had learned how to fly. In his dream, it was early October and the maples, oaks, birches, sumachs, willows, elms, beeches, and white ashes in the village were approaching the peak of their annual fall glory. He went out the back door of the old house, made his way past the apple tree where the now silenced ghost of the suicide victim dwelled, and scrambled through dense bush to the cliff-top summit of the steep hill at the back of his family's property.

From the top, he looked upwards at soft white clouds pierced by shafts of sunlight in the deep blue Muskoka sky and saw the face of Jehovah just as it was portrayed in his grandmother's illustrated Bible, together with those of his great-grandfather, the preacher, and his mother's cousin, the trapper. Looking downwards, he saw the Indian River, and out across its swift-flowing black waters, the locks and public docks. And approaching the docks was the *Sagamo*, the largest steamboat of its class on the smaller waterways of Canada and the pride of all Muskokans. The flagship of the Muskoka Lakes Navigation Company with four decks, triple-expansion steam engines, and capacity to carry eight hundred passengers, it was on its last outing of the season and carrying a full load of tourists anxious to see the fall colours up from the big cities.

An urge to join the images in the sky and the passengers on the *Sagamo* overcame the boy, and he willed himself to fly. The task seemed impossible at first, but eventually, to his delight, he managed to lift himself off the ground. Then, by concentrating with all his might, he moved forwards in the air off the cliff and out over the Indian River. Raising his arms, he soared effortlessly into and through the clouds again and again in a vain attempt to touch the images that melted, changed shape, and disappeared from view as he approached them.

When he looked downwards, he saw the village spread out before him with houses reduced to matchboxes, the main street to a ribbon, the swing bridge over the Indian River to a toy, the giant white pines at the Indian Camp to Christmas tree decorations, and the schoolyard to a postage stamp. And painted around these landmarks were the overlapping and vivid splashes of yellow, red, brown, orange, and scarlet of the leaves that would soon be blown from their branches by the rains and winds of the fall.

The air was fresh and clear, and there was not a sound to be heard, not even the rippling of wind as he effortlessly explored the heavens. An inner voice told him that humans could not fly and dreams were not supposed to be in Technicolor, but he ignored these messages and revelled in the freedom and intensity of the experience.

Then swooping downwards, the boy skimmed the waters of the Indian River like a swallow and landed lightly on the dock. A group of tourists standing on the deck of the *Sagamo* marvelled at his prowess.

"Who is that boy? Isn't he wonderful?"

Then a group of kids from the school materialized. Astonished at their classmate's unknown talents, they appealed to him to reveal to them the mysteries of human flight.

"It's easy," he told them. "You just have to believe you can do it."

But despite trying, despite closing their eyes and concentrating as hard as they could and despite leaping into the air and flapping their arms, they failed to take off.

The boy watched in silence for a while, walked calmly to the edge of the dock, and rose effortlessly above the housetops. After hovering for a moment, he took off down the Indian River without a backwards glance. With arms outstretched in the manner of Superman, he flew past the site of the deserted Indian settlement of Obajewanung, past the modest cottages of the less affluent summer residents, past the trailer camps, cabins, and campgrounds that in season were always jammed to overflowing with working-class families, past the elegant summer homes of the rich people from the big city, located a discreet distance from their poorer neighbours, past the mouth of the Indian River, and out, onto, and over the blue-black waters of Lake Muskoka itself, the preserve of the super-rich, until he saw off in the distance the sacred rock in the shape of the Indian head that was so important to the people of his mother's reserve and to Indians everywhere.

As he came closer, he saw that the god of the rock, normally so grave and reserved, was looking at him and smiling. A feeling of profound and overwhelming joy, happiness, and peace such as he had never before experienced overcame him. At that moment, however, he awoke, realized he had merely been dreaming, and cried tears of disappointment.

Entering the grounds of the school, the boy watched the other children at play but could think only of his dream. Instead of joining the other kids in the playground, he drifted into his classroom and stood staring out the window.

Suddenly he was the champion of the poor in far-off old England. An oppressive overlord had been levying harsh taxes on the peasants, leaving them without the means to feed and clothe their families. The boy, however, was sailing over forests, fields, and villages towards the castle of the evil baron. He would find the ill-gotten gold, take it away, and return it to its rightful owners!

Landing on the parapet of the castle, he forced his way past guards too astounded at the sight of the flying avenger to offer serious resistance, then entered the strongroom and picked up the treasure.

It was, he thought, amazingly light.

Returning to the real world, the boy saw that he had picked up a nickel from the desk of a classmate. Before he could put it back, the bell rang and the room flooded with children. He quickly put the money into his pocket, planning to return it at recess when no one would see him.

There would, however, be no more daydreaming that day for the boy. A fellow student soon had his hand in the air, waving it frantically to get the teacher's attention.

"Miss Sellers! Miss Sellers! Miss Sellers! Someone has stolen my nickel! I forgot it on my desk last night, and this morning it's gone!"

A deathly hush came over the classroom. Even Miss Sellers, a gentle yet firm red-haired young lady who had replaced the teacher who had held the boy back a year earlier, looked distressed and pale, for in the school stealing was a strapping offence. To make matters worse, the victim's father was the school principal.

This man had been hired over the summer by the stern Calvinist members of the school board to re-establish discipline in the school after his predecessor had left in disgrace, following an incident when the big boys in the high school had locked her in a broom closet. A large, powerful man in his mid-thirties much given to quoting Scripture, the new principal speedily established his authority. There were five rooms in the school and five teachers including the principal for grades one to twelve. He directed his colleagues to use the strap liberally on the children. They did, some more enthusiastically than others. The principal took the lead, but did not limit himself to the strap. He provoked the boys he wanted to expel from the high school by taunting them about their academic failings, by prodding them with a yardstick, by poking them with his fingers, and by slapping them around. When they fought back, he beat them with his fists, heaved them bodily out the door, and told them never to return.

Miss Sellers opened her desk drawer and took out the hated strap, a piece of stiff heavy leather, the length of a man's forearm, well-polished by frequent use on recalcitrant schoolchildren over the years. Placing on her desk the instrument of torture designed to leave welts on hands, wrists, and arms, she called upon the thief to come forward, return the nickel, and accept his or her punishment. The guilty party would, she promised, get off lightly. A mere three lashes on each palm; should there be any delay, the punishment would be very harsh indeed!

"Thief? Theft?" The boy was puzzled. "Why was there all this talk about stealing?" He had merely liberated a treasure to help the poor of old England! He knew, however, that there was no chance that the teacher would believe him if he tried to explain. Coward at heart, he had no wish to be strapped. He sat tight-lipped as Miss Sellers told the children that theft was a terrible thing and reminded them how important it was never to take property that belonged to others.

The boy agreed, but still did not want the strap. By this time the principal, scowling with self-righteous indignation, his body twitching with excitement as he contemplated the delicious prospect of thrashing another miserable delinquent, stood menacingly at the back of the silent desks. Just three weeks earlier, perhaps concerned that the other teachers were being too lenient, or perhaps because he simply enjoyed inflicting pain, he had begun strapping the children of the elementary school as well as those of the high school.

He had made a spectacular start when a child reported that a sandwich in her lunch bag, left in the hall outside the classroom, was missing. The principal decided instantly that the culprit was a good-natured, slow-witted girl in grade five who often had to go to the bathroom while the class was in session. Setting a trap, he put a candy on a sink in the girls' washroom and lay in wait in the mop closet. The girl took the candy and put it in her mouth. The principal pounced and dragged the screaming child back to her classroom. There he shook and berated her, calling her the lowest form of beast and a common thief. He then seized the strap already pre-positioned and ready on Miss Sellers' desk and administered a pitiless beating on her hands and arms, saying he would teach her something she would never forget.

"Let this be a lesson to the rest of you! Theft will not be tolerated in my school."

The boy was all too aware that if he owned up to his offence, the principal would likely take over the strapping duties from Miss Sellers and administer a punishment far harsher than the three promised lashes on each hand. He therefore sat silently, his heart beating so loudly he was afraid the teacher could hear it from the front of the room.

"If that is the way you want it, then so be it!"

The boy stared fixedly at his desk to avoid the angry eyes of his teacher. Too scared to think properly, he heard the voice of Miss Sellers wrapping up her exhortation in what seemed to him a voice of doom coming from afar. She was not, he knew, the oppressive baron of his imagination in the far-off old England but she was about to capture him and pronounce his death sentence.

One by one, the teacher called the children to the front of the classroom. One by one, the students were asked if they had stolen the money. One by one, they were asked to empty their pockets and then to turn them inside out in full view of the classroom.

The boy waited, petrified with terror. The money was in his pocket. He was about to be disgraced and strapped!

Finally, it was his turn.

"Did you steal the nickel? If you did, say so now or it will be really hard on you."

The boy looked at his classmates. They were now divided into two camps, those who had passed the interrogation and those who waited their turn. The first group were relaxed and smiling, looking forward to seeing someone other than themselves receive a good strapping. The second were nervous, aware that they were not guilty, but knowing there had been cases of injustice in the past, and even the blameless could find themselves in trouble.

"Well! Speak up! Did you or did you not steal the money?"

The boy said nothing. He now knew he had done wrong. It had, however, been for a good cause.

"Empty your pockets!"

He reached into the pocket where he had put the nickel. To his immense relief, he discovered that the nickel had fallen through a hole into the lining of his pants and down to lodge in his cuffs. Wordlessly, he turned his pockets inside out and stood looking innocently at Miss Sellers.

"Next!"

It was the turn of someone else, and the boy returned to his seat.

At recess, he retrieved the nickel and slipped back into the room. He put it back in the exact spot he had found it and fled outside.

"Miss Sellers! Miss Sellers! I have the nickel! It's back! It's back!"

The relieved teacher, who hated strapping children,

smiled broadly and left to pass the news to the principal, who had returned to his high-school class.

The boy was not the only one in his school with a fertile imagination. The favourite games of the elementary school boys had traditionally been cops and robbers, and Canadian commandos and Nazi thugs.

"Bang! Bang! You're dead! I gotcha!"

"No you didn't! I gotcha!"

In the evenings and on weekends, the sounds of battle could be heard throughout the village as boys ran from house to house aiming toy guns or their fingers at the bad guys. No one of course wanted to be either a robber or a Nazi. The boy and his best friend were enthusiastic participants in these wars. Happily, cowboys and Indians had gone out of style. Or perhaps, just possibly, no one wanted to hurt the boy's feelings.

The big boys in the high school smiled indulgently at the fantasies of the small ones. With the exception of one or two who joined in the games of their younger brothers and their friends, they had more serious matters on their minds. Many were talented hockey players, and one or two hoped to play professionally someday. A few intended to follow their fathers into the army or air force as soon as they were old enough. Several were hoping to go on to Teachers College. Most found the outdated and demanding course of study in which Latin was a compulsory subject and French was taught as if it were a dead language, impossible to master. They expected to drop out or to be thrown out by the principal without finishing their studies and then to find work in one of the myriad of local low-paying jobs in the tourist trade as apprentice carpenters, painters, electricians, or stonemasons. All of them hated the petty tyranny of the new principal and were plotting revenge.

"Who does he think he is anyway! No one should be treated that way!"

In the schoolyard and in the basement recreational room, resentment against the principal boiled over.

"When Hallowe'en comes, we'll show him."

On Hallowe'en, there was as always the breath of winter in the air, and the leaves had long since fallen from the trees. The boy and his best friend went from house to house as soon as it was dark, knocking on doors and crying "Trick or treat." The good-natured villagers laughed at their blackened faces and makeshift hobo costumes of ragged clothes topped off by masks. Everyone showered candy, fruit, peanuts, cookies, and gum on them and made a great show of trying to guess who they were. The boys left the homes where their identities had been ascertained in good humour and moved on without further incident to the next one. Where the occupants had no idea who they were, they ran behind the houses, pretending to be depraved goblins, soaping the windows, upsetting garbage cans, and hammering on the doors with their fists before fleeing, laughing like maniacs. Afraid of the principal, they steered clear of his house.

After tiring of collecting goodies and committing their minor transgressions, they drifted over to join the big boys smoking cigarettes and lurking in the shadows behind the school.

"Just you wait! Will he ever be mad! I can't wait to see the old buzzard's face at school tomorrow!"

The big boys, it turned out, had carefully planned a raid on the supplies of toilet paper stored at the school. Stealing the paper and using it to decorate the trees of the village, in addition to being great fun, would challenge the authority of the principal, infuriate and hopefully humiliate him. They had only to wait until the village constable grew tired of his Hallowe'en patrol and went home.

A large pear-shaped man with more fat than muscle, known affectionately as Old Jack, the constable ambled by, flashlight in hand, and did not see the plotters. Almost deafened by the battlefield roar of twenty-five-pounder guns during his service in the Royal Canadian Artillery in the war, he also did not hear them. Never married and old in spirit beyond his years, he lived in a furnished room provided to him free of charge by the members of the local branch of the Royal Canadian Legion in exchange for light custodial duties. Like other confirmed village bachelors, Old Jack wore – winter, spring, summer, and fall – long underwear that he scrupulously peeled off once a year for a washing, according to village rumour. He was also a creature of habit, downing a glass or two of beer every evening with other survivors of the two wars. It was the veterans' favourite time of day, for the old soldiers had vivid imaginations and they loved nothing better than to lard their memories of battle with extra detail, humorous anecdotes, and, as they sometimes laughingly said, "a few good lies" to improve a story.

After retiring to his room, Old Jack would prepare his dinner, adhering to a routine that he followed with military precision. According to the boy's father, who sometimes dropped in to share a beer with him in the evenings – and who it must be admitted loved to stretch the truth to improve an already good story – the constable would first remove his shirt to make himself comfortable. Next, he would sit down on his bed and think about the wonderful meal he was about to have. Then after a period of reflection – for he derived as much pleasure from thinking about his meal as he did in actually eating it – he would reach into a cardboard box under his bed and retrieve a can of pork and beans in molasses sauce, his favourite fare.

He would take it gently in his hand and look lovingly at the picture on the label. The picture – of a pot of beans heating on a stove – always brought back memories of the war, for beans had been one of the staple foods served up by army cooks. And thinking of the war always made him think of Betty Grable, whose tattered and much travelled photograph he had brought back from overseas and tacked to the wall above his bed. The Hollywood actress posing in a bathing suit to show off her superb legs (so valuable they had been insured by her studio, 20th Century Fox, for a million dollars) had been the pin-up of choice for American GIs and Canadian soldiers alike. Old Jack had followed the lead of his buddies and written away to Hollywood to obtain his very own autographed picture and taped it to his locker door in the British barracks where he and his fellow Canadians had been quartered before the invasion of Normandy. He had even carried it in his wallet when his unit went into action and fought the Germans across France into Belgium and Holland. And like his fellow soldiers, he had spent long hours gazing at her image, trying to imagine what he and she would do if they were to get together.

Sitting on his bed in his lonely room years later, Old Jack would glance up at the old photograph and remember that in those days he used to fantasize that

Betty Grable had come to Port Carling to see him after the war. He would propose they go dancing, but she would tell him she preferred the music of the newfangled big bands, such as those of Tommy Dorsey and Duke Ellington, to the square dance and Scottish Country dance tunes Old Jack knew and loved. He would suggest they go to the movies in the nearby town, but she would reply that, living in Hollywood, she had already seen them all. She would propose they cuddle in the back of a car, but he would be forced to tell her he did not own one. He would consider inviting her on a boat ride but would decide not to, since she would be embarrassed, he was sure, by his old rowboat when there were so many fancy motorboats driven by rich tourists on the Muskoka Lakes. He was certain, however, that she would want to share a good meal with him.

At this point in his recurrent fantasy, Old Jack's imagination would kick into high gear and back to food. He would see himself walking hand in hand with Betty Grable into Hanna's General Store and buying an enormous can of pork and beans from old Fred Hanna himself. With enormous smiles of satisfaction, they would return to the Legion, ignoring the envious looks of the old soldiers sitting at the bar. They would walk up the stairs to his room with Old Jack carrying the can for everyone to see and admire. They would open the can. Old Jack would offer her a fork and take another, and together they would eat from the can. Being a gentleman, he would suggest she consume all by herself the piece of high quality pork fat that is a standard feature in all cans of pork and beans. She would blush and then demurely accept.

The constable would then completely forget Betty Grable and think only of the beans. His mouth would water. Then after ten or fifteen minutes of great anticipatory delectation, growing hunger, and gastronomical arousal, Old Jack would reluctantly return to reality and focus on the hard decisions he now had to make to prepare his meal. And this was not as easy as you might think. First, he had to figure out which can opener to use. He owned two hand-held devices, and each had its advantages and disadvantages. One came with a sharp point at one end. It was easy to manipulate but dangerous to use. You simply employed brute force to impale the top of the can with the pointy end and then to saw around the circumference of the lid in short jerky movements. After completing the circle in whole or in part, you then pried the lid open. The problem was that short jerky movements left sharp jagged edges and there was always the risk that you could cut off your fingers in the process and leave them in the can.

The other opener was equipped with a variety of gears and a handle in the shape of butterfly wings. You merely squeezed the gears together around the rim of the lid and cranked the handle to turn the gears until in some mysterious way the lid was sliced off. No jagged edges resulted from this process but when the operation was finished, the lid usually fell into the can and became covered with molasses sauce. The constable hated fishing the lid out of the sauce, but faced with leaving his fingers or the lid in the can, he usually opted for the opener with the butterfly wings.

The other big issue was whether he should heat the beans on his handy hotplate or eat them cold. His dilemma was that he loved the sweet fulfilling aroma and taste of piping hot beans but hated the fuss and effort involved in turning on the hotplate, emptying the contents of the can into a pot, and waiting for the molasses sauce and slab of pork fat to begin to simmer; then, of course, he had to ladle his meal onto a dish, sprinkle it with salt and pepper, turn off the hotplate, spoon his meal into his mouth, and then wash pot, dish, and spoon. It was usually just not worth the effort, and on most nights he ate the beans cold and straight from the can, consoling himself with the thought that in the fighting in Northwestern Europe, he had often eaten his army-issue food that way with no ill effects.

Sometimes, as a treat, the old soldier would eat a can of Spam with his pork and beans. On particularly special occasions, he would put a can of Bartlett pears

– the kind that were cut in quarters and swimming in a light sugar syrup were his favourite – on the ledge outside his window for an hour to cool. Then, after finishing off his pork and beans and Spam, he would eat the pears. And with the pears, he never agonized over whether he should or should not eat them directly from the can. For when he removed the lid, the aluminium interior of a can of pears was revealed in all its glory, sparkling and glistening through the sugar syrup like the most polished and expensive silver dishes. Best of all, when he threw away the empty can, he knew that he could count on obtaining the same sensual joy just by opening another can.

The constable was invariably in bed and sound asleep by ten o'clock. He slept with a clear conscience. Despite living in a small room in the Legion, having neither wife nor children to keep him company, having no one to cook hot meals for him and to wash his clothes, he was a happy man. He was at peace with himself, had his memories of good wartime service to his country, and had a job that he loved. Although in a position of authority, Old Jack was well liked by everyone, including the children of the village. In contrast to the principal, it never would have occurred to him to strike a child.

And true to form, that Hallowe'en night the affable constable sauntered into the Legion shortly after nine o'clock, looking forward to a glass of beer, good conversation with his buddies, and a meal of pork and beans, and did not re-emerge. Confident they would see no more of him, the big boys went to work. First, they boosted one of their number up to a window that someone had surreptitiously unlocked during school hours. He slipped inside and disappeared into the dark. A minute later, he opened the back door to admit his co-conspirators. Silently entering the building, they quickly descended the stairs to the basement furnace room where the school materials were stored. A few minutes later, they came back out, each happily carrying a large box of toilet paper. They had hit it lucky. A year's supply had just been delivered to the school, and they had more than enough to festoon the leafless trees of the village with fluttering white garlands.

The boy watched the action in a daze. After living through so many adventures in his imagination, he was now a spectator to a real commando operation. The older boys carrying the boxes of toilet paper were transformed into rebellious American colonists extracting cases of tea from the hold of a ship in Boston Harbor at the beginning of the American Revolutionary War. In a flash, the colonists became pirates looting a Spanish merchant ship in the Caribbean. Then as the pirates began throwing roll after roll of toilet paper into the black and bare branches of the maple, oak, and birch trees lining the main street, they became American marines hurling satchel charges of explosives and hand grenades into the pillboxes of Japanese soldiers fighting to the death on Iwo Jima. And he was the lucky witness to it all!

The next day the school principal, looking grim and unpleasant as always, gathered the students together. The boy feared the worst. Had the principal found out who had liberated the storeroom of its toilet paper? Was he about to punish the entire student body? Would there be expulsions? Did the principal know he had been at the scene of the crime? Would he get the strap and the public humiliation he had dodged during the incident of the nickel?

Instead the principal smiled.

"The village looks beautiful this morning, students. Congratulations on your artwork. But you boys should have seen what my friends and I used to get up to on Hallowe'en when we were your age! What you did was nothing in comparison!"

Perhaps, the boy thought, the old brute was not so bad after all.

SEVEN

—

The Entrepreneur

IN TIME, THE BOY EMERGED from his fantasy world and became obsessed with making money. But not for miserly purposes. He had no interest in hoarding wealth and no wish to become rich. He simply wanted to treat himself to ice cream cones, comic books, and the occasional bottle of pink cream soda. And these treasures cost a dime each, a fortune in the spring of 1950 to the boy, who was now ten years old.

How was he going to earn the money to obtain such luxuries? At first, it did not seem particularly difficult. Thumbing through a copy of the *Family Herald*, the most popular weekly magazine in rural Canada at the time, he saw advertisement after advertisement outlining how easy it was to make money fast. His main problem, it seemed, would be to decide which offer to select from among the many being made by selfless businessmen, all of whom, for a modest outlay of capital, of course, wanted to share their secrets of money-making with the wider public.

A "sure-fire plan to make millions" by manufacturing and selling cedar oil was particularly attractive. For only one dollar, a kind businessman promised to send instructions on the industrial process involved and to purchase all the oil produced. The boy was excited, since there were plenty of cedars out back of his house and in the swamp behind the dump. He would soon be rich!

Another one undertook, in return for only thirty-five cents, to divulge the secrets of raising red hybrid worms in profusion to sell for bait. The boy was particularly interested in this offer since he already had some experience in the bait business.

The year before, he had nailed a sign advertising "Fine Muskoka Bait Worms for Sale Cheap" on the wild cherry tree near the highway at the bottom of the steps leading from the old house. He had, in fact, no worms to sell but intended to remedy that problem by collecting them when they emerged on rainy days from their holes on the big lawn in front of the old hotel uptown beside the locks and swing bridge. He also planned to dig for them in the manure pile at the farm of his best friend's uncle. But somehow that never happened. When it rained, he didn't want to get wet. And on sunny days, he didn't like the smell of the manure. He had, however, never discouraged the tourists who came by looking for worms. His answer was always the same.

"Jus' sold the last ones. Try again tomorrow."

He also encountered interesting people. The highlight was meeting Barbara Ann Scott, winner of the gold medal for figure skating at the 1948 Winter Olympics at St. Moritz, Switzerland. The famous figure skater was the heroine and sweetheart of Canadians young and old, and from coast to coast, and the photograph of her landing a double lutz was a fixture on the front pages of newspapers and magazines. Commentators praised her beauty, talent, determination, and ethical purity. Her feat in winning the gold medal on a slushy, uneven, skate-scarred outdoor rink just after a hockey game – not to mention her decision to turn down the offer of a new car from the city of Ottawa to conform to the spirit as well as the letter of her Olympic oath – had become the stuff of legend unequalled in the annals of Canadian sports lore, at least until Team Canada beat the Russians in the Canada-Soviet hockey series of 1972.

The boy would never forget the moment of his brush with greatness. He was sitting on a rock under the sign advertising his product, chewing on a piece of timothy hay, reading a comic book and lost in thought as always when a car pulled up.

"Excuse me, little boy, could you sell me a dozen worms?"

The boy looked up and was about to tell the potential customer to come back the next day when he saw, to his astonishment, that it was Barbara Ann Scott herself, smiling at him from the passenger side of the vehicle. His heart almost stopped, and instead of answering, he rushed up the steps and burst into the old house.

"It's Barbara Ann Scott! It's Barbara Ann Scott! She wants to buy worms! Come and see!"

His brother and sister rushed out and accompanied him to the car while his mother came out to take a peek from the front porch. Barbara Ann smiled and asked for her worms.

The children, tongue-tied, merely stared. Canada's sweetheart left, perhaps wondering if Port Carling was inhabited by a race of morons.

After due consideration of all the options, therefore, the boy decided to make his fortune in cedar oil and red hybrid bait worms. All he had to do was to find one dollar and thirty-five cents.

As he reflected on how he would raise his start-up capital, the boy saw that there were many other opportunities listed in the classified section. And you did not have to send money. In sales, for example, the astute and far-sighted could go door-to-door selling boxes of magic tricks, used military clothing, square dance outfits, costume jewellery, ladies' nylons, laying chickens of all kinds, Bibles, Bible prophecies, snowshoes, food flavours, oils, greases, paints, plaid flannel, second-hand school desks, cosmetics, fully grown ringneck pheasants, name plates, fragrant deodorizers, cigarettes from Egypt, fire extinguishers, and reconditioned gas refrigerators.

It was also possible to start a mink ranch and deal in furs, raise Siberian huskies and sell puppies, start a pig farm and market Landrace sows and boars, open a ranch and invite the public to come riding, start a business removing bark from dry pulpwood logs, and establish a chicken farm and raise White Leghorn hens. You could also take correspondence courses to be a hairdresser, to decorate cakes, to be a draftsman, to become a skilled auctioneer, and to acquire the skills of a concert pianist. And most intriguingly, the sufficiently motivated could become an expert on stopping "feather-picking and cannibalism in chicken flocks" – whatever that meant.

There were other great deals. Just by writing, a boy could get a free sample of an ointment "guaranteed to relieve painful itchy piles and eczema," hair cream "to make you look twenty years younger," a booklet on how to get rid of pinworms, a special product to remove ingrown toenails, tonic tablets to make you gain weight, and a colour brochure describing a revolutionary new chimney design.

Canada was truly a country of opportunity. The boy did not understand why so many people were poor. Obviously, they did not read the classified section of the *Family Herald*.

Over a seven-day period, he carefully prepared letters in his scrawling handwriting to every one of the businesses, farms, educational institutions, and other organizations and individuals advertising in the *Family Herald*. His message was simple.

Dear Sir,
I am interested in your offer in the *Family Herald*.
Please send information.
Yours Truly,
Jimmy Bartleman

He then laboriously wrote his name and address on the top left-hand corner of each envelope and took the pile to the post office. With no money to buy stamps, he simply stuffed the lot of them into the mail slot and hoped for the best.

The boy's immediate priority was now to find one dollar and thirty-five cents. Fortunately, the paper boy in the village for the *Toronto Daily Star* was retiring. Actually he was just a kid two years older than the boy, and he had grown fed up with lugging his load of papers through rain, sun, sleet, and snow to thirty demanding customers along a four-mile route.

The *Toronto Daily Star* had the largest circulation of any newspaper in Canada and embraced the most progressive causes. It had in its storied past featured outstanding journalists, including Robert Service of *The Cremation of Sam McGee* fame, known internationally as "the Canadian Kipling." Ernest Hemingway and Morley Callaghan were other *Toronto Daily Star* alumni. Hemingway, of course, was the Nobel Prize winner for literature and author of *For Whom the Bell Tolls*. Callaghan was Canada's most celebrated writer of short stories and was famous for having challenged and knocked down Hemingway in a boxing match in Paris in the 1920s.

Gordon Sinclair was another lead columnist. Although not world renowned like Hemingway or Callaghan, he was very well known in Ontario. As roving reporter in the 1930s, he had sent back fascinating and lurid accounts in that pre-CNN world of his encounters with Japanese warlords in China, Buddhist monks in Burma, and French prison guards on Devil's

Island in French Guyana. Some of them seemed almost too dramatic to be true. He had then either been fired or had retired from the *Toronto Daily Star* to become the opinionated host of a talk radio show in Toronto that was popular in Muskoka. He still wrote guest columns and was well known in the village since he had a cottage in the area.

None of this impressed the outgoing paper boy. His beef was that Canada's leading newspaper was simply too heavy for him to carry.

The *Toronto Daily Star* had in fact been growing in bulk for some time. Its arch rival was the *Toronto Telegram*, with which it had been fighting circulation wars for years. It had always emerged victorious, and as a consequence attracted more advertising than its competitor. A *Toronto Daily Star* customer could thus obtain twice the number of pages at the same weekly rate as a subscriber to its rival. And this did not even include the heavy weekend supplement, the *Star Weekly*. This was good for the *Toronto Daily Star* but bad for the paper boy in Port Carling.

"If you want this stupid job, you can have it."

The boy made some rapid calculations. Although not particularly strong in mathematics, he was able to figure out that he could earn enough in only one week to send away to the *Family Herald* for the secrets to making a fortune in cedar oil and red hybrid worms. There would even be money left over. He wanted the job.

In due course, the world-weary district circulation manager for the *Toronto Daily Star* came to the door of the boy's house. He was responsible for hiring boys in the towns and villages of Muskoka to deliver Canada's heaviest newspaper, and fancied himself to be a keen judge of youthful character.

"You can make five cents a customer each week! There are prizes galore! All you have to do is to find new customers!"

He handed over a glossy catalogue showing spiffy telescopes, powerful flashlights and fishing equipment.

"For every new customer you find, you get so many points. When you have accumulated enough points, you get a reward."

This was even better than the boy had imagined and he signed up on the spot.

The boy was soon able to send one dollar and thirty-five cents to the *Family Herald*. The holders of the secrets on how to get rich fast with cedar oil and red hybrid worms, for some reason, never replied, although they did keep his money.

In response to the boy's broadside mailings, however, dozens of letters and product samples flooded in, proposing all manner of business deals with the Port Carling entrepreneur. The initial reaction of his father was to laugh, and he congratulated his son on putting one over on the city slickers in far-off Montreal, where the *Family Herald* was published. He found it less funny, however, when a succession of sincere business people appeared in the village, asking to talk to the local magnate interested in collaborating in their ventures. All, with the exception of a couple of representatives from the company selling the revolutionary new chimney design, did not tarry after they saw the boy's business address. The two salesmen, who had come all the way from Toronto, sat down on the old couch with drinks in their hands and talked for hours to the boy's hospitable father about their product and the prospects of marketing it in Muskoka. Then again, perhaps they just wanted to enjoy the raisin wine.

The boy decided to forgo get-rich schemes and to concentrate on making money from newspapers. His start was excellent. He went from house to house recruiting new customers, starting with prominent villagers who subscribed neither to the *Toronto Daily Star* nor to the *Toronto Telegram*. He refused to take no for an answer when these householders said they were not interested.

"But look at whatcha kin git if you take out a *Toronto Daily Star* subscription: international news, hot crime stories, and the best comics of any newspaper in

Canada! And Gordon Sinclair from down on Lake Muskoka still writes for it."

Embarrassed and irritated, his prospective customers were forced to tell the wheedling, persistent youngster that they had never learned to read.

"Now leave us alone!"

The boy backed off and turned his attention to the clients of the *Toronto Telegram*. They at least knew how to read and would not be able to get rid of him by admitting they had learned nothing from their years at school.

And by not taking no for an answer, he managed to persuade six long-term subscribers to switch their business to the *Toronto Daily Star*. They would soon regret their decisions. The boy in turn received as a prize a flashlight, complete with batteries, from his impressed circulation manager.

His performance from that point went steadily downhill. His intentions were good. Each afternoon, he ran home from school, eager to start his deliveries. Each afternoon, a load of newspapers, bound with wire and dumped from a truck at a corner close to his home, awaited him. Each afternoon, after cutting the wire, the boy would close his eyes and inhale the intoxicating smell of fresh newsprint. And each afternoon, he would not start his deliveries until he had read the newspaper from cover to cover.

After scanning the headlines, he would turn to the comics section. He particularly liked *Li'l Abner* since he could identify personally with the country bumpkin hero of the dysfunctional Yokum family. In fact, the Muskoka he knew was not all that different from the Dogpatch of cartoonist Al Capp. Individuals in Port Carling were spitting images of the bossy Mammy, the insipid Pappy, the voluptuous Daisy Mae, and the loveable, outrageous Hairless Joe. His own family house, unpainted, lopsided, and with tarpaper on the roof and an outhouse in the backyard, looked for all the world like the Yokum residence. The only difference was the Yokum privy came equipped with a door decorated with a cut-out half moon, while his had no door at all.

The boy would then turn to the sensational stories of murder and robbery that were the lifeblood of the *Toronto Daily Star*. A woman in Port Carling was married to a Toronto gangster, and with a sense of civic pride he watched for his name when lists of criminals were published. At that time, the most infamous felon in the country was Edwin Alonzo Boyd, a former soldier turned bank robber. His exploits were so daring, Canadians considered him to be their own Jesse James. It was the boy's secret hope that the bad guy with the Port Carling connection would make it big by joining Boyd's gang. He eventually did so, to the boy's delight, but got caught and was sent to the Kingston penitentiary. The boy would end these reading sessions by carefully going through the paper, checking for anything he had missed, whether advice to the lovelorn, letters to the editor, traffic accidents in downtown Toronto, horoscope readings, the weather, births and deaths, sports, or the latest sales at Eaton's.

It took time, of course, to go through such a big newspaper in its entirety, especially on Saturdays when the *Star Weekly* appeared with its extensive comics and short story sections that he could not wait to read. With the outbreak of the Korean War in June, it took him even longer to complete his evening reading. A copy in his hands, he would sit hunched over on his pile of newspapers and study the maps printed on the front page outlining the shifting battle lines. The news was always bad that first summer as South Korean and then American forces fell back in the face of North Korean military superiority until they were bottled up in a small defensive perimeter in the south, and commentators began to predict that the war was lost. And with such momentous news from half a world away, it was not surprising that he would lose track of time.

In those days before the coming of television, his customers relied on newspapers for information on world developments and they were furious when they were forced to wait longer and longer for the dawdling youngster. On Friday evenings, when the boy sought payment for his deliveries, they took him to task, pointing out that his predecessor had provided much better service. And when they handed over their thirty-cent weekly subscription fees, no one gave him a tip. One short-tempered old-timer, who had become angrier and angrier as he waited for his newspaper, went so far as to chase him down his driveway but failed to catch him.

Another customer, an enormous, red-faced, hard-drinking trucker much given to beating his wife and kicking around his own children, warned the boy he "would be in fer it" should he not "straight'n up." The boy paid him no heed. One Friday night, so late it was already dark, the disgruntled and violent client was lying in wait. As his wife looked on, smiling thinly, he closed the door to the kitchen after the boy entered the room seeking to be paid for the newspapers he had delivered that week.

"Kid, I told yuh yuh'd be in fer it if you didn't straight'n up."

The boy ducked behind the wife as the glowering trucker came stumbling after him. She stepped to one side to make it easier for her husband to seize the youngster, but the boy kept her between him and his pursuer.

"C'mere, you dirty little half-breed, I'll larn you to pay attention to what I say."

The trucker lunged at the boy, coming so close that he enveloped him in his foul, beery breath, but he could not catch him. They played a grim game of hide-and-go-seek around the bewildered wife for what seemed like an eternity to the boy, with the trucker bellowing curses and constantly grabbing for him.

The boy then made a break for it, darting out of the kitchen into the living room and out the front door to freedom. Heading for home, running as fast as he could into the night, he discovered that his troubles were not over. As he ran, he heard the engine of the old dumptruck parked in his customer's driveway cough once and come to life. His persecutor had followed him out the door, climbed into his vehicle, and despite fumbling around in an alcoholic haze, trying to put the key in the ignition, had succeeded in starting it and switching on the headlights.

Manipulating the stickshift was more of a challenge. There was a clashing of gears until the trucker found the sweet spot, slipped the vehicle into reverse, and backed it out onto the highway. After a momentary pause, accompanied once again by the sound of grinding and growling in the transmission, he shifted awkwardly from first to second and then to third, at the same time pressing the accelerator to the floor and sending his ancient truck shuddering down the road.

In later years, and in another world and life, the boy, then a man, would think of the truck and its headlights when he first saw at the Reina Sofia museum in Madrid

Pablo Picasso's great epic painting *Guernica* and its depiction of a demented and tortured horse being punished and pushed beyond its limits by forces beyond its control. For in the imagination of the frightened youngster on that night in Port Carling so long ago, the headlights of the dumptruck piercing the gloom – jerking first up and then down as the truck lurched forward after him – were the illuminated wild eyes of a demented, supernatural equine monster determined to chase him down and stomp him to death.

In a panic, the boy dove into the ditch, closing his eyes as tightly as he could and shoving his face into the dusty ferns, dandelions, leaf mould, twitch grass, and burdock covering the damp, cool ground. Covering his ears with his hands, he willed himself to become invisible in an irrational attempt to escape once and for all from his tormentor. In an instant that was an eternity, waves of sound and light rolled over him – and on down the road as the truck sped by, leaving him in the comfort of the silent darkness.

Scrambling to his feet, the trembling boy slowly realized the trucker was no longer after him. For it was Friday night and on Friday nights, he remembered, his unhappy customer had more important things to do than trying to run down defiant *Toronto Daily Star* paper boys. On these evenings, he got together discreetly with two buddies in a room behind the meat freezer at the butcher shop to play poker, to smoke cheap wine-dipped cigars, to drink rye and ginger ale with beer chasers, and to eat pickled eggs, pickled pig tails, and pork rinds. It was not a merry gathering. There were no good-natured jokes, and no one sang "Frankie and Johnny." Instead the trio, in language laced with foul invective, spent their time complaining about everything and everyone – spitting with disgust on the sawdust-covered floor whenever they wanted to emphasize particularly telling points.

Summer residents from the United States "who swaggered around the village as if they owned it," lazy Indians, "furriners" smelling of garlic, women with moustaches and unshaven legs, good-for-nothing teenagers, noisy children, indulgent parents, the state of the public wharf, barking dogs, sanctimonious preachers, welfare bums, potholed roads, spotty garbage collection, farmers who let their livestock run loose, licentious actors from the big city, crooked politicians in Toronto and Ottawa, and the inhabitants of a nearby village who got drunk in public, bought fancy cars yet lived in tarpaper shacks, played dirty hockey, attended fundamentalist churches, and married their first cousins – these were the usual targets of their scorn and wrath.

The boy knew all this since he was privy to the secrets of the butcher shop. The butcher's helper was his friend. An orphan waif scooped up from the streets of an English slum some forty years previously, he was one of the tens of thousands of impoverished children transported across the ocean in the late nineteenth and early twentieth centuries by Barnardo Homes, a British charitable organization, and placed with families across Canada. The goal of Barnardo Homes was to provide a fresh start and the hope of a better future for the destitute British children. More often than not, however, farmers took in "home children" simply to obtain unpaid labour, and treated them badly.

Such was the case of the short and scrawny butcher's helper, who in addition to having to suffer as a home boy, had been born with one leg shorter than the other and with a heart condition. After leaving the care of his foster parents, he had found it difficult to find steady work. Despite not having the money to pay for expensive medical treatment in those days before universal medicare, and being able to afford no better accommodation than the leaking one-room cabin he rented from his employer, he bore his burdens stoically. Having suffered so much himself and being kindhearted by nature, he was always ready to do a good turn to someone in need.

And what the boy needed was offal to feed his family's malamute huskies. For more than a year, therefore, the helper had been allowing the boy to collect the scraps of meat, fat and guts left on the floor or tossed into a box after sides of beef, pork, and mutton had been cut up and chickens, ducks, and turkeys killed and eviscerated. The three hardened drinkers had become used to seeing the boy pawing through the bloody garbage for food for his dogs. They had paid him no attention, and the nosy boy had not missed a word of their bitter commentary.

All three – middle-class members of the village's respectable drinking caste – would eventually die of alcoholism, but not before suffering attacks of delirium tremens that drove them from their sickbeds into and through the streets, their frantic families in pursuit, ranting about flying elephants, pink dragons, devouring monsters, and in the case of one of them, no doubt, recalcitrant, ineffective *Toronto Daily Star* paper boys. But the youngster did not know that at the time. And even if he had, he would not have cared. All he wanted to do was to reach the sanctuary of his home, where no adult had ever lifted a hand against a child.

The boy's mother, seeing the fear in her son's eyes when he dashed into the house, asked him what was wrong.

"Ain't nutt'n wrong. Jus' wanted to get home before it got too dark."

The boy was determined to fight his own fights and not to worry his mother. He dealt with his violent customers by cancelling their subscriptions. He stayed clear of the trucker on Friday nights by going early to the butcher shop to collect his scrap meat, well before the three drinkers started their morose weekly get-togethers. To the other disgruntled clients, he said if they did not like the service he provided, they could take their business to the *Toronto Telegram*.

None did. And despite their unhappiness with their new paper boy, several well-intentioned people tried to give him good advice.

"Many of Canada's biggest businessmen got their start delivering newspapers. Mend your ways, young man, and maybe you too will go far."

The boy took their guidance to heart, at least initially. He went with his mother to the Port Carling branch of the Bank of Nova Scotia and with great ceremony opened his first bank account. He intended to deposit the ten dollars and eighty cents he received each week from his customers. He intended to write a cheque each week to the *Toronto Daily Star* for the nine dollars due to it. He intended to leave ninety cents, one half of his earnings, in his account. He intended to give his mother the other ninety cents to help out at home.

His mother was proud of him, and the bank manager shook his hand. The boy then learned just how difficult it was to reconcile his different priorities. It was summer and Whiting's Drugstore and Ice Cream

Parlour opened its doors for the season on July 1. And Whiting's, as confirmed by its out-of-date advertising, sold all manner of fascinating things.

> *Dealer in Drugs, Patent Medicines and High Class Toilet Preparations. Souvenirs, Grass Goods and Indian made Porcupine Quill Boxes. Also a select stock of Moccasins, Fishing Tackle, Magazines. Williard's Forkdipt Chocolates, Neilson's Pure Ice-Cream, fresh daily, and fruits in season. Large dancing surface where you are always welcome, and Tea Room upstairs where homemade dainties are served. The Store Where Quality Comes First.*

After collecting the weekly payments from his newspaper customers on the first Friday of July, the boy, his pockets heavily laden with nickels, dimes, and quarters, entered the store.

Behind the counter was the proprietor of the establishment, Big John Whiting himself. Tall and massively built with white hair, a sallow complexion, enormous jowls, and a huge paunch that hung down over his belt like a sack of wet cement, he had been a dour fixture of village summer life since well before the Great War. A cheap cigar with a long ash at the tip was clamped firmly between his yellow teeth and smoke drifted out of his nostrils and mouth. He stared at the boy through glasses with lenses so thick they resembled the bottoms of Coca-Cola bottles and magnified his cold blue eyes to look like giant bugs of uncertain origin.

Waddya want, kid?

The boy dug into his pocket, proudly pulled out a handful of change, and carefully selected a dime that he plunked down on the counter.

"Gimme a pink cream soda, please."

Big John smiled with grim satisfaction as he handed over the ice-cold bottle. He could recognize a weak-willed client with money to burn when he saw one.

And he was not mistaken. For after satisfying his craving for the sweet, vanilla-flavoured carbonated drink – available in Muskoka only at Whiting's in the summer months – he turned to the tubs of ice cream, zeroing in on the butterscotch. Surely he deserved one small cone after all the work he had done?

Big John was ready to oblige and served up a butterscotch cone. One cone, however, led to another. Soon the now happy proprietor was serving butterscotch, maple walnut, strawberry, and raspberry ripple double-decker cones to the boy, who licked, sucked, and munched his favourite ice cream varieties to his heart's content. And as he gorged himself, he drifted over to the magazine rack and stared at the comic books.

"I kin afford to buy one *Batman*. But look! The latest *Superman*, *Little Orphan Annie*, and *Dick Tracy* have arrived! And wow! Whiting's is now carrying Classic Comics! There's *Kidnapped, The Swiss Family Robinson, Robin Hood*, and *The Man in the Iron Mask*. I just hafta have them. They're educational. My mother would like that. And I could always trade them with the kids at the Indian Camp!"

Thus the boy began his descent into ice cream and comic book addiction. He bought one comic book and took it outside, cone in hand, to read at his leisure on a bench on the public wharf. It was heaven on earth to be ten years old, flush with cash on a hot summer night in Muskoka, savouring the taste of melting ice cream, and inhaling the distinctive, intoxicating odour possessed only by brand new comic books. In the background, on benches of their own, he could hear old Indian war veterans, several his own kin, gossiping in Chippewa as they always did at that place and at that time of day. There was the sound of water lapping against the mahogany sides of expensive motorboats moored to the docks, the buzzing of mosquitoes, the fluttering of moths against outdoor light fixtures, the explosive strafing of dive-bombing night hawks attacking flying insects, and the musty, oily smell of old dock planking nailed to creosote-soaked cribbing.

Two hours later, he was still sitting at the same place. There was a stack of comic books piled up beside him on his bench, his hands and lips were sticky – and Big John had relieved him of all his money.

And try as he might, the boy could not break free of the vicious circle. Like an unreformed junkie, he was hooked and could not, would not, and did not change his ways. Every Friday night until summer's end, he made his way to Whiting's Drugstore and Ice Cream Parlour, where Big John provided him with ice cream and comic books in exchange for the money his customers had paid him for their newspapers. So shameless did he become that he even offered his mother an ice cream cone and comic book for her birthday, knowing full well she would give them back to him. By midsummer, he had become enormously popular with his friends at the Indian Camp. He also had a growing debt at the *Toronto Daily Star*, and had given no money to his mother.

But just when matters risked getting completely out of hand, the circulation manager of the *Globe and Mail* came to his house. Home delivery of the *Globe and Mail* had never been established in Port Carling, since in those days it was the newspaper of city folk, and the locals had no interest in it. The *Globe and Mail* was, however, available during the summers in a rusty newspaper box on the main street. A member of the company's management board, who had a summer home in Muskoka, took note and was most unhappy. He issued a decree to his company's circulation manager in Muskoka.

"The *Globe and Mail* is Canada's national newspaper and is the most influential in the country. Some of the most powerful people in Canada are summer residents of Port Carling. It is not fitting that they should obtain the *Globe and Mail* from some miserable box. We must hire an experienced and energetic paper boy to sell it on the public docks to people who are used to receiving it at their homes in the city."

The circulation manager, told by someone in the village that the boy delivered the *Toronto Daily Star*, assumed that he was experienced and responsible and asked him to take on selling Canada's national newspaper as well.

"It would only be for the rest of the summer. You can easily handle the workload. Sell the *Globe and Mail* in the mornings and make your regular deliveries of the *Toronto Daily Star* in the evenings."

The boy once again made some rapid calculations. If he could sell thirty copies of the *Globe and Mail* daily at five cents each for six days each week, he would take in nine dollars. He could use the proceeds to pay off his debts to the *Toronto Daily Star*. Once that was done, he would use his returns from the *Toronto Daily Star* to pay the *Globe and Mail*. He was becoming a real whiz at mathematics.

He signed up immediately, and his mother, who knew nothing of his machinations, was ever so proud of her industrious son.

But the boy grew tired of walking the docks each morning in search of influential Canadians. Why not subcontract the sales of Canada's national newspaper to an already-existing business?

He approached the proprietor of a small gift shop on the main street.

"I have the monopoly in Port Carling on the sales of Canada's national newspaper, read by the most influential of people. I am prepared to let you have all my newspapers, and all you have to do is to pay me the full price of five cents each. You will not make any money when you sell them, but people who cannot live without the *Globe and Mail* will buy other things when they come to your store."

The proprietor could find no fault with the boy's logic, and accepted his offer. For the rest of the summer, the boy was paid in full for the *Globe and Mail* newspapers he no longer had to sell. The proceeds, he gave to the *Toronto Daily Star*. And he used his earnings from the *Toronto Daily Star* to buy ice cream cones and comic books.

Being in business was not all that difficult, he thought. Or at least until summer's end on Labour Day when the circulation manager for the *Globe and Mail* came to his house. The boy saw him pull up in his car and fled out back and hid behind the woodpile. His mother answered the door.

"I have come for the money owing the *Globe and Mail*."

"What money? Haven't you been paid?"

"No, we definitely have not been paid. But that's not the real problem. We wanted the *Globe and Mail* sold on the docks of Port Carling for perfectly good reasons. Instead, your son has betrayed our trust by selling his copies to a gift shop. Had I known, I would never have hired him."

The mother came to the back door and called for her son to come inside and explain himself. He did not budge.

"He's not here."

The mother went to the jar where she kept her husband's wages and paid the boy's bill without further comment. After the departure of the circulation manager, her son emerged from hiding, and she said that she was ashamed of him.

EIGHT

—

The Father

THE BOY'S PARENTS WERE disappointed when he disgraced himself by juggling his newspaper accounts to pay for comic books and ice cream cones. After her initial reproach, his mother said nothing further, but he knew she felt let down. His father, however, had lashed out.

"Good gawd, boy! Wake up to the fact you're alive! If you don't watch yourself, you'll grow up to be just another lazy Indian."

The boy knew he deserved a reprimand but felt his father had been unjust. Did he mean his son was tainted with some inherent defect because of his Indian blood and would never amount to anything in life, no matter what he did? A seed of doubt about his own capacities was planted that he would never completely overcome.

And was his father a hypocrite, being friendly to Indians but not meaning it? In his heart of hearts, the boy was certain his father was not a racist. He had reacted blindly, resorting to the language of the village in the process, and had not meant what he said. The boy recognized, however, that he had to redeem himself.

The process of reconciliation started in the fall of its own accord after the departure of the last of the summer residents. Despite having only a few years of schooling, his father had always loved reading and had acquired a mastery of the written word that he never employed in speaking, but that he used to penetrate the mysteries of books in all their varieties. When the lighting in the house had come from smoky coal-oil lamps, he had found it hard to indulge his passion. After the house was wired to the grid and the lighting came from electricity, he began to frequent the small village library, borrowing books to satisfy his thirst for literature – translations of French classics by Victor Hugo and Alexandre Dumas, Zane Grey Westerns, novels by John Steinbeck and Pearl Buck, Harlequin romances, and accounts of the early exploration of Canada by Alexander Henry, Samuel Hearne, and La Vérendrye. The boy, who up to then had read only comic books and newspapers, turned his attention to the books his father left lying around the house.

One evening early in the fall, his father departed for the library and the boy followed behind. It was already dark, and there was no one on the streets. Afraid of being told to go home and not to bother him, the boy stayed well behind as his father led the way past the locales where so many of the small dramas that had loomed so large in the short life of his son had been played out. He went by the United Church where the boy attended Sunday school, proceeded past the butcher shop where he collected scrap meat for his dogs, and crossed the swing bridge over the Indian River, close to the Indian Camp – the boy's summer-time hangout – which was hidden in the darkness across the water and deserted at that time of the year. He then pushed on up the hill in front of Stephen's grocery store where the boy had sabotaged the tires of the grocery delivery truck and past the homes of villagers who waited impatiently each evening for him to deliver their copies of the *Toronto Daily Star*. From half a block away, the boy standing in the shadows watched his father enter the library. Once his father was inside, he approached the well-marked door.

Port Carling Public Library
Open Tuesdays and Thursdays 7 to 9
Saturdays 2 to 4

Afraid that only adults were admitted, the boy worried that he might be expelled but decided to give it a try. Taking a deep breath, he turned the handle and went in. His father, already thumbing through a book, glanced up at him with a small smile and carried on as if his son was not in the room.

The kindly librarian, however, smiled at the youngster who stood hesitantly inside the door and beckoned him to join her at her desk. She explained the mysteries of library use and gave him a short tour of the stacks, pulling books at random from the shelves to let him know what was available. Many of the books, the boy saw from the inscriptions on the inside covers, were old novels, biographies, and boys' adventure stories donated by cottagers over the years. She then issued him a card, valid for three books at a time and told him to be sure to come often. And when the father left the library with his quota, he was accompanied by his son with three books of his own – and whose universe from that day on was no longer confined to his village.

That first evening, father and son read late into the evening, the father on the old couch and the boy at the kitchen table. The only sound in the room was the rustling of pages. The father was lost in a novel by Hugh Garner, one of his favourite Canadian authors who wrote about the life of down-and-out workers riding the rails during the Great Depression and scratching out meagre livings in the slums of Toronto, while the boy was immersed in the adventures of *The Swiss Family Robinson*. The Swiss clergyman, his wife, his four sons – Fritz, Ernest, Jack, and Francis – ranging in age from six to fourteen, together with their fierce dogs – Flora and Turk – had managed to escape their shipwrecked vessel and had made it to shore with a supply of fishing hooks, fowling-pieces, bags of powder and shot, and were about to start their new life on a deserted island. Because the boy had already read the classic comic book, he knew how the story would unfold and his mind wandered; none of the guys he knew at school read books, and he wondered what they would think of him if they learned that he had joined the library. He decided he didn't care.

He began to feel sorry for his father, forced to work at labouring jobs for starvation wages and yet more knowledgeable about books and better informed about world developments than the fathers of his friends and the prominent villagers who did not even know how to sign their names. He asked himself if he would turn out like his father, well-read but impoverished. His mother, sensing that a bond was developing between father and son over literature, let him stay up long past his bedtime. Exposed to the real thing, the boy never returned to comic books.

Their relationship was further strengthened later that fall when father and son became poaching partners. For after the departure of the summer residents, the local people hunted and fished out of season. Each October, before the start of "hunt'n" season, men and boys armed themselves with rifles and shotguns and killed every moose, deer, bear, fox, raccoon, rabbit, squirrel, chipmunk, partridge, goose, duck, crow, and chickadee they could find. When they were not killing live animals, they got together for "turkey shoots" or marksmanship contests, in a field back of the dump, with freshly slaughtered turkeys donated by the village butcher as prizes. In those weeks, the sound of gunfire was the background music of village life. Occasionally the villagers shot each other or themselves – accidentally, of course.

The boy's best friend, bored with using tins cans for target practice, even shot his aunt's cat. He quickly and secretly buried the poor animal in her backyard before she found out and told his father. The cat was a beautiful, two-toned tortoiseshell tabby, an excellent mouser called Puss-Puss, much loved by her mistress. For weeks, the aunt put out saucers of milk each evening in the hope the cat would come back. Each night, an enterprising raccoon would drink the milk, keeping alive hope in the distraught lady's heart that her pet was still alive. She scoured the neighbourhood every day, calling for Puss-Puss to come home and visited the houses of her neighbours, including that of his best friend's parents, asking that they watch out for her kitty. The friend, who lived in dread that a fox or dog would dig up the cat and reveal his crime, quietly removed Puss-Puss and reburied her back of the dump.

The boy, armed with his .22 rifle and accompanied by his best friend, took part in the general slaughter, although he shot no cats. When he felt the need for heavier armament, he borrowed an ancient double-barrelled, twin-triggered, ten-gauge shotgun from his friend's father. With this weapon, he hit nothing other than the tops of trees, since the blast of the sixty-year-old black-powder ammunition, which came with the gun, was so powerful the barrel jerked upwards each time he pulled the trigger. He once pulled both triggers by mistake. The resulting detonation drove the stock with a hammer blow into the youngster's shoulder and chin, rendering him semi-conscious and knocking him flat on his back with his feet in the air – to the delight of his best friend, witness to the spectacle.

By the time the *official* hunt'n season opened, the villagers had purged themselves of their need to shed blood for another year and had hidden away in cold storage lockers all the wild meat they required for the winter. Of course, they still went to their hunt'n camps.

Every year, the majority of the village's able-bodied men abandoned their jobs, garbed themselves in red jackets, armed themselves with .303 rifles and twelve-gauge shotguns and departed the village in a convoy of creaking horse-drawn farm wagons loaded with baying hounds, axes, saws, coal-oil lanterns, bedding, tin cups and plates, fire-blackened pots and frying pans, and cases of canned food and drink – in short, everything deemed essential to survive for two weeks in the wilds of the Georgian Bay hinterland. Smiling women and children and teary-eyed and rheumatic old-timers itching to participate but too infirm to go lined the streets to wave goodbye to the brave warriors. The annual ritual, unknown to the public outside the district but just as important to the people of the village as the most ancient ceremonial parades are to the inhabitants of similar small communities in rural areas of Europe, was as spectacular as it was deceptive. For the real goal of the hunters was to hide deep in the bush, drink beer and liquor, eat pork and beans, pickled eggs, and hot pepperoni sausages and play cards out of sight of their wives until hunt'n season was over.

The boy's father never went hunt'n because he couldn't afford the expense, did not play cards, was a vegetarian, and loved animals.

The hunters returned to the village in mid-November. After giving themselves a few days to take baths, sober up, purge their bodies of all traces of pork and beans, pickled eggs, and pepperoni sausages, shave their beards, have their hair cut by Mel Wallace at his barbershop, tell tall stories about all the animals they almost shot and try to remember the latest raunchy stories they had heard while playing poker, they turned their attention to the poaching of fish.

And fish, the boy's father arbitrarily and illogically decreed, were not animals since they were cold-blooded and did not suckle their young. With no qualms about catching or eating them, he joined enthusiastically in this village sport.

"Fish'n" at that time of the year was always good because it was spawning season. In addition to being strictly forbidden legally, it was also morally wrong to take advantage of fish trying to lay eggs. But traditions were traditions, and the men of the village were creatures of habit. Their fathers and grandfathers had preyed on spawning fish; if their descendants did not follow in their footsteps, they would be guilty of sullying their memories. Every year, therefore, the men carefully removed spears and nets from their secret hiding places, lovingly restored them, and went fish'n in the dark of the night.

Different skills and technologies were employed by spearers and netters. Spearers would glide quietly in their canoes to the shoals, shine strong lights on the fish preoccupied by their lovemaking on the gravel bottoms, and impale them with their barbed lances. Even among the most hardened poachers, however, spearing was considered somewhat disreputable, given the horrible injuries inflicted on the fish.

Netters were more respectable. They employed gill nets that looked like spiderwebs hanging down into the water with floats on the top and lead weights on the bottom. They, too, used canoes but had no need for lights. They simply let their nets out over the shoals and allowed the unsuspecting fish to swim into the webbing and become entangled. The technology was so simple and so effective that it had long been banned in most lakes of the province. Those arrested risked a massive penalty – a one-thousand-dollar fine and confiscation of net, boat, and vehicle.

In Muskoka, however, the chance of being caught only added to the thrill. And in Port Carling, the local game warden, in addition to doing a roaring business as the village bootlegger, enjoyed breaking game and fish laws as much as anyone else. And with him onside, the villagers did not worry unduly.

Year after year, therefore, the men set their nets under the cover of darkness and returned before dawn to harvest their catches of pickerel, lake trout, and whitefish to share with family and friends. The boy's father had been accepted as part of this outlaw fraternity shortly after arriving in the village. His closest fishing partner was an industrious and intelligent young graduate of the Port Carling high school who was getting some practical experience in poaching before reporting for training as a RCMP constable at the Regina Police barracks. This exposure to the dark side served him well; in short order he would rise to the top ranks of the RCMP. And as a good parent, the father allowed his boys to help out, sometimes taking them with him in his nighttime forays.

Everyone in Port Carling was, of course, aware of these goings-on. The families and close friends of the poachers were kept well-supplied with fresh fish. Those outside the circle, however, especially the elderly and shut-ins, received nothing. The boy saw an opportunity to do a good turn and to make some money.

"Why not let me sell fish to my newspaper customers?"

He told his parents that in so doing, he would be keeping alive a noble family tradition. When his mother was a child at the Indian Camp, she had sold door-to-door in the village the fresh fish caught by her father. After his marriage to his Indian wife, his father had fished with his Indian in-laws and sold the catch to tourists. When the case was put to them in this way, the parents were proud of their son for endeavouring to follow in their footsteps. His newspaper customers were delighted when he delivered fish as well as copies of the *Toronto Daily Star* to them in the evenings. His prices were reasonable. He even took orders and gave the proceeds to his parents as a sort of peace offering for his bad behaviour of the previous summer.

This bliss came to an end when game wardens from the outside, tipped off that their colleague in Port Carling was in cahoots with poachers, raided the village, armed with a list of suspects early one evening in late November. The boy and his brother were sitting at the kitchen table listening to the *Fibber McGee and Molly* show on the radio. Fibber McGee, as usual, was down at the Smackhart General Store describing to his skeptical friend, Throckmorton P. Gildersleeve, his latest outrageous scheme to make a fortune. Their father, as was usual after dinner, was stretched out on the old couch, engrossed in a book.

The brother saw flashing red lights in front of a neighbour's house.

"It's the game warden!"

The father leapt to his feet, raced to a shed behind the house, grabbed the net, and fled with it into the bush. After hiding it in a secure location, he returned to the house to await the law. Similar scenes were being enacted throughout the village as word spread of the arrival of the game wardens. Eventually, the game wardens came to the door of the boy's house. They were happy because they had just arrested the neighbour next door after finding a gill net, frozen fish in his freezer, and fish entrails and scales in profusion in his garbage. Self-righteous with the justice of their mission, eager to display their authority, and looking forward to arresting yet another lawless poacher, they flashed their badges to intimidate the family and brandished powerful flashlights to help them in their search for evidence.

"We have reason to believe you have been netting fish, and have a warrant to search your house."

"Me? Never! But you are welcome to come in."

They found nothing. The net was safely stowed deep in the bush. The family did not own a freezer to store fish and by happy chance the boy had delivered the remaining stock of fresh pickerel to his customers earlier that evening. The game wardens likewise found no evidence when they poked their way through the garbage, for the family never threw fish heads, scales, and other offal away. It was given to the malamute husky sled dogs, family pets that were used to haul wood home from the bush in the winter and were kept tethered behind the house.

These dogs had no intention of co-operating with the Law. They lunged, fangs bared, at the game wardens when they shone their lights on them. The officers decided to forgo examining their quarters. Had they looked in the boy's newspaper bag, they would have found old wet newspapers covered in fish slime and scales. It would have been sufficient, perhaps, to convict someone. But they did not.

The boy's mother decided that the risk of being caught was too great. Were her husband to be convicted, the family would never be able to pay the one-thousand-dollar fine, and he would have to go to jail. Then who would provide for the family? She gave the net to one of her cousins on the reserve and brought to an end the boy's opportunity to share illicit fishing experiences with his father.

NINE

—

The Voices of the Pioneers

By this time, the boy, aided by the special ties he developed in delivering poached fish, had rebuilt his relations with his newspaper customers. To provide prompt service, he now read the *Toronto Daily Star* after rather than before beginning his delivery rounds. And on collection nights, always inquisitive, he would ask the old-timers, the children of the pioneers, why their families had come to Muskoka in the first place and what they remembered of the Indians. The old people, naturally hospitable and somewhat lonely, loved to talk about the old days, and began to invite him in for hot chocolate and cookies.

"Lad, our parents wuz lied to."

They then regaled him with stories of hope, disappointment, and endurance. Canadian government agents in the old country in the latter half of the nineteenth century had, in fact, misled the first settlers, inducing them to come to Muskoka by offering them two-hundred acres of land free of charge and claiming that the land was excellent for farming. All the prospective landowners had to do was to remain on the land they picked out for five years and fulfill a certain number of conditions, and it would be theirs.

A flood of enthusiastic people took up the offer. They left their homes in England, Scotland, and Ireland to brave the violent waters of the North Atlantic, to journey up the St. Lawrence River to Montreal, passing the villages and towns settled by French colonists as long ago as the early seventeenth century. Then they travelled by train through towns and cities such as Cornwall, Kingston, Belleville, and Whitby, populated in more recent times by immigrants from the United States and Britain, to Toronto, then a city of sixty thousand. There they purchased guns, axes, clothing, cooking utensils, and other items judged necessary to prepare them for life in the backwoods of the province. It was then onwards north by rail to the end of the line at the town of Barrie at the southern tip of Lake Simcoe, where they embarked on a steamboat to travel to the head of the adjoining Lake Couchiching.

Up to this point, the emigrants had passed through long-settled lands and encouragingly prosperous farms and villages. The old-timers said their parents fully expected that after a few difficult years of clearing land in Ontario's frontier country, they would soon be planting crops in deep, lush soil and joining the ranks of Canada's comfortable farming class. But they were to be disappointed.

On disembarking, the hopeful pioneers found themselves standing in dense bush and being attacked by clouds of pitiless mosquitoes and blackflies. Roads as they had known them in the old country did not exist. To reach their destination, they first had to pass through an immense cedar, alder, spruce, and hemlock swamp, over a so-called Corduroy road of logs laid at right angles to the direction of the trail over the mud. Then they had to navigate the grandly named Muskoka Colonization Road – actually a rough stump-studded track that threaded its way through the white pine, beech, oak, and birch wilderness uplands and over ridges and alongside beaver meadows to the bottom end of Lake Muskoka. Until a railroad and a functional highway were pushed through, the early settlers had the choice of walking or of riding in bone-jarring ox carts and stage coaches that often became mired in the mud.

In short order, the pioneers discovered that the agents in the old country had neglected to mention that the soil in most places was limited to a thin covering of leaf mould on top of glaciated pre-Cambrian granite. Nor had they referred to the heavy snowfalls and the bitter cold of endless winters, a growing season so short the leaves began to change colour in late August, or to the primitive accommodations of rough, dirt-floored shanties, the monotonous diet of sowbelly pork and molasses, the backbreaking labour required to clear land, and the crushing isolation and absence of stores, schools, churches, and doctors. No one warned them that women with peaches-and-cream complexions acquired in the moist, mild climate of Britain would be turned in short order into gaunt, worn-out, hollow-eyed drudges, their lifespans shortened by frequent pregnancies and constant child rearing as well as endless labour in fields, stables, and homes. They were not told that those lucky enough to find patches of arable land among the lichen-covered boulders and bedrock to cultivate crops would more often than not have to carry their wheat on their backs in heavy sacks over rough trails to be ground at a distant mill – and have to bring the flour home the same way.

They even failed to tell them that there were Indians in the district at the time, let alone that these native people might think they owned the land they had occupied for so long.

The old folk would smile as they complained, because they were justifiably proud of what their fathers and mothers had accomplished despite their hardships. Their parents, they pointed out, had followed in the tradition of the earliest pioneers in pushing back the frontier and creating a modern, prosperous Canada. Just a few years after the arrival of the first settlers, enterprising businessmen started a steamboat service on the Muskoka Lakes, facilitating the movement of freight, merchandise, and people. A dam, public docks, and locks were built at the site of the rapids on the Indian River around which the future village of Port Carling would grow. Logging companies moved in, hiring local men and boys to harvest the giant white pines that dominated the landscape, thereby injecting cash into the local economy. Husbands and sons drowned working on the lakes, or were killed in lumber-camp accidents, but their families just carried on. Middle-class Canadians from the big cities in the south streamed into the area on fishing and hunting trips, eventually purchasing land and constructing cottages. Wealthy Americans from Pittsburgh then adopted Muskoka, building palatial summer homes on the islands.

As a result, the first settlers, who were leading subsistence lives with no markets for the products of their bush farms, for the first time found people anxious to buy their fresh milk, butter, eggs, poultry, lamb, pork, and beef. Soon the more enterprising among them were opening small hotels. A number of these places grew in a generation to become huge, luxurious establishments for the well off. Before the end of the century, tradesmen had started building canoes and rowboats to sell to the summer residents.

And by the start of the Great War, a couple of inventive villagers formed the Disappearing Propeller Boat Company. Known affectionately as Dippies, the boats were actually heavy skiffs or rowboats with retractable propellers and shafts powered by lightweight gas-powered engines. In short order, since people liked the idea of protecting their propellers in shallow water, the company was the biggest motorboat company in Canada. Within a decade it folded, but the old-timers never forgot their moment of motorboat glory.

Then in the early 1930s, disaster struck the village. The boy did not need the old-timers to tell him the story, for his mother, then a girl of seven living with her parents in their one-room shack at the Indian Camp, had been a witness to the traumatic developments. She told her son that fire after fire had mysteriously broken out in those years, systematically torching the main buildings of the business section. She remembered waking one December night in 1930 to the frantic pealing of the church bells in the Presbyterian church, calling on every able-bodied villager to form a bucket brigade to fight the fire that would destroy the main boatworks of the community.

Then, the next fall, she heard the bells again, and as her father rushed to join the volunteer firefighters, she stood with her mother on the shore of the Indian Camp and watched flames and explosions light the night sky. Hanna's General Store, then a large wooden building filled with lumber, cases of canned goods, boxes of soap, drums of gasoline, tins of paint, and all manner of flammable materials in its basement storeroom, burned to the ground, and the fire spread from building to building until the entire business section with the exception of one hotel, the Port Carling House, was a smouldering heap of ashes. But the people just rolled up their sleeves and started again, this time erecting fine brick fire-resistant buildings and endowing the village with a business section vastly superior to those of surrounding communities of similar size.

The old-timers were proud of the pluck and accomplishments of their fellow villagers.

"You ain't gonna find a more up-to-date and purdy village of its size in all the Dominion. We got street lights, town water, our own telegraph office, a party-line telephone exchange, our own school, a nice natural ice-hockey rink complete with a change room heated by a box stove, a community centre dedicated to our war heroes, a library, and in the summers a restaurant and the Straw Hat Little Theatre, with big-shot actors all the way up from the big city. And now there's even talk about putt'n in sewers! And to think a hundred years ago this place was just bush!

"Today, Port Carling is the village in the district with the greatest community spirit by far. The Legion and the Lions Club are going strong, and there's never any shortage of volunteer firefighters. Even the Orange Lodge has lotsa members here, even though it's fadin' fast elsewhere in the Dominion. And that's a great shame because there was a time not so long ago in this here province of ours when every village, town, and city had its own Orange Lodge and Orange Hall. Anyone who was anyone – whether reeve of this village, mayor of Toronto, or even prime minister of the whole country – were members of the Lodge. It used to be the real centre of community life in this here village. At one time, even the English Church held its services in its hall. It still has high ideals despite what some people say about it. Thank gawd, the people of Port Carling have remained true and faithful."

The boy knew something about the Orange Lodge. At the urging of his best friend who came from a strong Orange Lodge family, he had attended a meeting of village youngsters, who were being recruited to join the youth movement of the organization. On that particular evening, no one talked about high ideals. Instead, the youth leader had quickly reviewed the history of the organization, dating back to the defeat of Catholic

James II by Protestant King William III at the Battle of the Boyne River in Ireland on July 12, 1690. The boy then had to sit through an uncomfortable evening as the leader and other speakers ranted on about the perfidy of Papists, the venality of priests and nuns, and the inferiority of French Canadians. Having himself been at the receiving end of bigotry, the boy could hardly wait to get away. And when he got home, he had to endure a tongue-lashing from his father, who was strongly opposed to the Orange Lodge and all that it stood for.

The boy was puzzled at the hatred he encountered that night, a sentiment he assumed was shared by his elderly customers, for there were no Catholics and no French Canadians in the village. There was one small community up the lakes where most of the people were English-speaking, French-Canadian Catholics, but they enjoyed excellent personal relations with everyone in the village, including the Orangemen. He assumed the old-timers would not take kindly to discussing the matter with him and said nothing. They had been raised in an era in the province when anti-Catholicism and prejudice against French Canadians were part of the popular culture. As a generation, they seemed to be set in their opinions and determined not to let their personal friendships affect their deeply held beliefs.

He reckoned, however, that he would be on safer ground in probing the old-timers about the native roots of the village and the aboriginal people who had spent their summers, year after year, for most of the past century down at the Indian Camp. Indians, in contrast to Catholics and French Canadians, had never been the object of long-term systematic vilification by the leading fraternal organization of the village. Yet in response to his questioning about the Indians who lived in Obajewanung, the old-timers were not particularly forthcoming. Yes, there had been a community of Indians at the site of the future Port Carling when their pioneer parents had arrived. Yes, the Indians had been hospitable when the first settlers had arrived uninvited and unannounced, and had provided them with food and seed corn and any help they could from their limited means. Yes, the Indians had been ordered to leave to make way for their parents. Yes, there were still a few Indian log cabins around when they were growing up. Yes, in fact, their families had appropriated some of the cabins for their own use. Yes, there were a few Indian burial grounds here and there, the locations of which had long been forgotten.

When the boy asked them if what their parents had done was fair, they admitted that the Indians undoubtedly had been treated badly. But, they added, the white people who built Port Carling were as deeply attached to their twentieth-century community as the Indians had been to their village when the settlers arrived. Their parents had made something out of Port Carling. If the place had been left to the Indians, they said, it would have been just another backward reserve. As far as they were concerned, the fact that Port Carling had once been Obajewanung was a mere historical curiosity and a closed chapter.

The old-timers were more comfortable talking about the Indians who came from the distant reserve of the boy's mother. They admitted that the settlers thought they were rid of Indians when the people of Obajewanung were expelled. They were surprised, therefore, when other Chippewas from farther south quietly appeared in the summers to erect their wigwams and tents around the locks and dam, telling them their ancestors had fished and hunted for hundreds of years in the area. These natives were soon joined by Protestant Mohawks from Oka, Quebec, who had moved to Muskoka after losing out in a land dispute with the Catholic church in the late nineteenth century. Initially, the natives spent their summers fishing and trapping, but they soon found a ready market for their handicraft among summer residents and day trippers from the steamboats. But the white villagers of the time did not like it.

"Our parents didn't want a bunch of squatters on prime land at the height of the tourist season."

The government, nevertheless, established a small reserve for them on several acres of land on the shore opposite the locks – and the Indian Camp was born. The old-timers confessed that relations between the two peoples had never been easy. To their knowledge, villagers and natives had never intermarried – the language and cultural gap between the two peoples was just too great. Besides, they said, there had been too many wild parties down at the Indian Camp for the liking of the villagers.

Aware of the boy's ties to the native world, they also tried to find nice things to say about the people in the Indian Camp and its inhabitants.

"The Indian Camp was a favourite with tourists who had never seen Indians before. It drew them to Port Carling. There even used to be wresl'n matches down there on Sundays. Some of them Mohawks were professionals and put on good shows. Everyone from the village and lots of tourists would go. There was one old fellow who was more than a hundred when he died. Was supposed to have met the old Queen herself . . . was a member of the Salvation Army, a great Christian, and leader of his people . . . was always down at the Indian Camp . . . always liked jawing with him."

One old couple, whose son had been killed in the war, remembered the contribution of the Indians in the wars.

"In 1914 and again in 1939, a lot of the guys down at the Indian Camp signed up. They made sacrifices just like our sons and were treated badly afterwards."

And, to the boy's delight, they told him they had known and liked his Indian grandfather.

"He was a hard worker. Got along with everyone and pitched in and helped us fight the fires of the thirties. Even entered a burning building and carried out a badly burned young lady from the big city who was spending the summer in the village. It was not his fault that she was so far gone she died."

But like old people everywhere, talking and joking about the good times of their youth was what they really wanted to do.

"Our parents had it tough, but people pulled together in those days. Everyone got together for bees to raise barns and houses. They got all the food they could eat and pailfuls of whisky to drink. No one asked for money. The men used to form teams and see which one could get the most done. And after the bee, they'd celebrate and fight all night."

"In the old days, we used to hold big sports competitions on Victoria Day and invite everyone around the lakes to come and try to beat us. There'd be rac'n, wresl'n, and jump'n. Trying to catch a greased pig was always great fun. In the winters, there'd be hockey, and the guys from Port Carling would win the fights if not the games."

"A rich man in my day was someone who could afford a two-hole outhouse rather than a simple one-holer!"

"You'd think the kids of today invented Hallowe'en. Why, when I was a boy, we'd wait until someone was comfortably sitting on the seat in the old outhouse before tipping it over. Once, after dark, we moved an outhouse a few feet down the path, just far enough to leave the honey pit unprotected, and then we hid nearby to wait for the fun to start. Sure enough, someone came out to use the facilities, didn't notice we had moved it, and just as he reached for the door, fell into the hole. He warn't hurt, but you should have heard the shout'n, holler'n, and laff'n. My gawd, now that was what we called hav'n a good time in Port Carling in the old days!"

"We even put a wagon full of hay on the school roof. And those guys who think they're so good at nett'n fish! Why, in my day, we used dynamite!"

"When I was a young man in the 1890s, there warn't no rules against drink'n and there was a bar in that old hotel down at the locks. Whisky was a dollar a gallon. The drink of real men was whisky and ale, half and half. As for the fight'n, it was Ulstermen against French Canadians every parade day on the Glorious Twelfth of July, the anniversary of the victory of Good King Billy in the Battle of the Boyne. It was Ulstermen against Ulstermen every weekend, and Ulstermen and French Canadians against Englishmen every night."

Their eyes misted over at the thought of the old days before the villagers went soft, built three churches, banned alcohol sales, and started catering to an upscale tourist crowd.

TEN

—

The Woodcutter

FROM OCTOBER TO APRIL, THE family's main worry and priority was heating the old house, for the building was poorly insulated, and the climate in Muskoka was severe. Prevailing winds from the west blowing across the Great Lakes dumped enormous quantities of snow each year on the highland district. The first frosts arrived in late September, the leaves were off the trees by mid-October, and the snow was on the ground to stay in early November. Temperatures in January and February often dipped to sub-arctic levels. Waist-deep snow would accumulate on the roof of the old house and giant icicles would build up under the eaves of the uninsulated roof, often reaching down to touch the ground. The highway would be walled in by high banks of pure white snow, and during heavy snowfalls cars and trucks that were unable to mount the steep hills of the village would be abandoned by their drivers until the snowplough and sand truck from the nearby town came through. And the ice would still be in the lakes, and snow would linger in the bush until April.

The stove was the first line of defence. Everyone shared the responsibility of stoking it with wood from the time the father lit the fire in the morning until the family went to bed. During the day, it was the centre of family life. A pot of nourishing barley soup, its flavour enhanced by marrow-filled beef bones, simmered constantly on one of the back lids. It was a rare weekend when there was not an apple or raisin pie in the oven. Johnny-cake, made from cornmeal, egg yolks, shortening, sugar, and baking powder, and served with corn syrup, maple syrup, or molasses, was often on the table. Baked beans, prepared from well-soaked white beans, onions, mustard, brown sugar, tomato sauce, and bacon were another favourite. They were eaten hot out of the oven or consumed cold with raw onions and salt and pepper in heavily buttered sandwiches.

The mother kept a large kettle of water constantly on the boil on Mondays for the weekly washing of clothes, pouring the hot water into a large galvanized steel tub filled with shirts, long underwear, pants, and other articles of clothing of the working-class family of six. After soaking everything in soapy water, she would get down on her knees, plunge her hands into the tub, take each piece in turn and vigorously rub it against the scrub board until all stains had disappeared. Then, after rinsing the clothes in fresh, clear water, she would wring each item as dry as she could with her hands, don hat, coat, and boots and bring everything outside. Standing on the stoop, she would pull the clothesline towards her and peg on the damp clothing. The articles of clothing would freeze, and as they froze, underwear, shirts, and pants would thrust out their legs and arms defiantly, sway in the wind, and take on the shape of stiff, menacing scarecrows. Somehow the next day, after she shook off any accumulated snow from the clothes and brought the load into the house for ironing, everything would be dry.

On Saturday nights, the mother filled the same tub with hot water for the children's baths, which were always taken to the sound of Foster Hewitt, Canada's most famous sports broadcaster, excitedly providing play-by-play descriptions of Toronto Maple Leaf hockey games from Maple Leaf Gardens in Toronto. Like everyone else in the village, parents and children alike were fanatical fans of hockey in general and the Maple Leafs in particular. In those years, they expected their team to win the Stanley Cup, and with the help of legendary players such as Turk Broda, Howie Meeker, Max Bentley, and Gus Mortson, they often did.

In the evenings, the boy often sat close to the stove, and with firelight from cracks along the imperfectly fitted doors glistening on his face, thought of the passing of time. The subject had been a preoccupation, almost an obsession, for as long as he could remember in his short life. Years earlier, before his family moved to Port Carling, his Scottish grandfather had come to fetch him at his home in the Southern Ontario town where his father had found work as a steelworker during the war. Grandfather and grandson, only five years old, had journeyed by rail to Toronto, where they changed trains at the old Union Station. They then proceeded to Orillia, the hometown of his grandparents, where he would spend several weeks.

It was afternoon in the sweltering heat of late June 1944 when they set off on their journey. The boy, dressed in a sailor suit provided by his father's sister, herself serving in the Royal Canadian Navy in far-off Halifax, stood for hours at the open window of the train, hypnotized by the rocking of the passenger cars on the railbed. Periodically, acrid smoke and grit from the steam engine chugging away somewhere up ahead, swept in through the window. The sweating passengers sharing the compartment took out rumpled handkerchiefs to rub their eyes, blow their noses, and cover their mouths as they cleared their throats. There was a grind of steel-on-steel and a rhythmic clickety-clack of wheels on track, interrupted by the slam of air from passing trains, the clanging of bells, and the wail of the whistle as the engine approached level crossings.

When they reached Toronto's Union Station, it was crowded with thousands of soldiers, sailors, and airmen. The boy did not know it at the time, but the final push to free Europe from Hitler had just begun. Canada's armed forces were in the thick of the fighting in Normandy, and casualties were heavy. All the boy could see as his grandfather led him by the hand across the marble floor of the Great Hall were black boots and legs in khaki and navy blue and air-force blue uniforms as servicemen and servicewomen hurried to reach their units or to take last-minute leave before reporting for duty.

As he stared at the flickering flames more than five years later in the heart of Ontario's cottage country, the boy dwelled not on these details but on the setting sun he had followed through the window of the train that day of early summer. He had watched it race behind telephone poles, farmhouses, and trees and yet never move. The five-year-old had puzzled over how such a thing was possible. The ten-year-old understood – or thought he did. The memory of the racing, unchanging sun made the boy wish his life and that of his parents would never alter. He was happy sitting in the security of the old house, enjoying the heat thrown by the stove, and he wanted that happiness to last forever. He knew, however, that his parents, even if they were younger than those of his friends, would grow old and die. And he would grow old and die. Why couldn't his family, he asked himself, like the racing sun on that day so long ago, change and yet remain the same and live forever?

The fire in the woodstove would die out an hour or two after the family went to bed, and heat would leak outside through the uninsulated walls and single-pane glass. The temperature inside would fall to subzero levels, and a coating of frost would build up on the windows. The soup on the now stone-cold stove would freeze, and the milk in the icebox would turn from liquid to ice, expanding and pushing up through the neck of the bottles in which it was contained. Water from the tap, left running day and night to keep the pipes from freezing, would splash on hitting the bottom of the sink and freeze in concentric circles. The icicles that dripped so profusely during the daylight hours when heat from the house penetrated the thin roof, would freeze rock-solid. The father's raisin wine, however, accorded immunity against freezing by its high alcohol content, would escape unscathed from the ravages of the cold. Upstairs, the family slept cozily in their beds, covered by warm blankets and wearing the long underwear they donned from November to April. And in the mornings, the children would wait to hear the roar of the freshly kindled fire, then emerge from beneath the covers and rush downstairs, clothes in hand, to dress beside the stove.

Christmas was a particularly joyous time that December of 1951. The family had carved out a place for itself in the village, and the mother had made the final payment on the old house and now owned it outright. On December 24, a large turkey, ordered from the butcher shop, sat on a table near the sink. On the opposite side of the room was the tree, a well-proportioned balsam fir, decorated with silver artificial snow, ornaments, electric lights, and with a star on the top.

The boy was proud of the tree, for he had cut it and hauled it home himself. In fact, he and his best friend had gone together with their axes and a bucksaw to a swamp back of the dump and felled a dozen spruce and balsam fir trees, reserving two for their own families and peddling the other ten door-to-door to neighbours for a dollar each. The work was crushingly hard, especially for boys of their age and size. The snow was deep in the low-lying frozen bog, and the only trees available were giants that dominated the landscape. The boys thus had first to stamp down the snow around the bases of the trees to give themselves room to work. They then notched the trunks in the desired direction of the fall and used their saw to cut through from the other side until the prizes came crashing down. Afterwards, they lopped off the crowns and dragged them out of the bush to sell.

They had asked the permission of no one. They had no idea who owned the land. Villagers had been obtaining their Christmas trees at this place for so many years that everyone had come to believe they had a right to take what they wanted.

On Christmas Eve, therefore, all was well in the boy's home. The fire in the stove was blazing, the woodbox was full of dry hardwood, holiday music was playing softly on the radio, the room was cozily warm, and the odour of Christmas cookies baking in the oven filled the house. The father was sipping from a glass of raisin wine and telling his children stories from his days riding the rails and working in lumber camps during the Great Depression. The mother was making last-minute preparations for cooking the Christmas dinner, and the boy was running his fingers through the five dollars in loose change that he had earned from his share of the Christmas tree sales. He had also turned eleven that day and had received a present from his mother and a birthday card with a one-dollar bill inside from his grandmother.

There was then a knock on the door. The father's eyes lit up. While he was prepared to keep on telling his stories to his own children, he craved the company of adults, who would drink with him, listen to his tall tales, tell their own stories, and best of all, joke and laugh with him into the night. He was hoping that one or more of his buddies had remembered him and was dropping by to spend the evening.

It was, however, a very different visitor, the good-natured United Church minister on a very different mission. Normally, the father would have muttered an excuse, put on his coat, and left the house to avoid talking to him. But now, inspired by the spirit of Christmas, and desperate for a new victim to listen to his stories, he greeted him warmly, asked him to join him on the old couch, and offered him a glass of raisin wine. With a smile, the minister courteously declined but accepted a cup of tea from the mother. For the next half hour, he listened politely as the father related story after story of his life "on the bum" during the Great Depression, including a few *risqué* stories, warmly appreciated by his son but not ideal for a clergyman. From time to time, the minister glanced uneasily at the turkey and other food on the table by the sink and at the richly decorated tree.

The good man, who had given the impression that he was afflicted with a problem difficult to resolve ever since entering the room, finally stood up and awkwardly explained the purpose of his visit. The members of the congregation had pooled their resources to provide the makings of magnificent Christmas dinners as well as presents for the families and children of needy villagers. The boy's family was among the lucky designated recipients. That said, he would now like some help to carry the packages from his car to the house.

The boy immediately volunteered his services. He knew his parents had bought and hidden away presents for their children, but he was eleven and would not say no to receiving even more. His mother and father, however, said nothing. For even if they had always been poor, they had never considered themselves to be so. Their working-class status they considered to be a mark of honour, and they were proud of what they had accomplished in the few years they had been in the village. They had never accepted charity in the past and certainly had no intention of accepting it now, however well-intentioned. After a long pause, the mother said the gesture was appreciated but there were families in the village far more needy than hers.

The minister, his face red, said he suspected that might be her reaction. And with a final glance at the turkey and the bountiful fixings of the next day's meal, he hastily made his escape. After he left, the whole family burst out laughing.

Shortly thereafter, there came another knock at the door. A tall, unsmiling Provincial Police Officer, flashlight in hand, hardly gave the mother time to say hello before he began his interrogation.

"Your son has been selling Christmas trees, has he not?"

The boy thought he was in deep trouble. The Provincial Police were rarely seen in the village and were usually called in only to deal with the most serious crimes, or to back up the village constable when the problems he was facing were too great for him to handle. The owner of the swamp, he assumed, had discovered that someone had chopped down a dozen of his largest spruce and balsam fir trees, and, not trusting Old Jack to conduct a vigorous investigation, had asked the Provincial Police to find the culprit.

The mother said nothing and did not ask him in. The policeman planted his boot in the door to keep it open and continued:

"Don't try to cover up for him. I know for a fact the young delinquent was peddling Christmas trees all over the village today. Someone cut down a prize blue spruce on the lawn in front of the cottage of one of the area's most important summer visitors, and it was probably him."

The boy breathed more easily. Someone else had swiped the blue spruce.

The boy's father got up from the old couch, joined his wife at the door, and asked the policeman what proof he had to implicate his son.

"Nothing in particular," was his answer. "But I'd like to take a look at your tree."

The father told him to go away.

The policeman stepped inside anyway, saw that a balsam fir and not a blue spruce graced the corner, and left without a word. The family did not laugh this time.

From a very young age, the boy had been expected to help out around the old house, preparing kindling and keeping the woodbox filled. Now in the winter of 1951, in light of his exploits harvesting Christmas trees, his father judged him old enough to help him cut firewood in the bush itself. Other families in the village bought their firewood from commercial distributors or paid the owners of wood lots to let them harvest trees from their holdings. The boy's father could afford neither. Likewise, he neither owned a truck nor had the money to rent one. In the early years, he cut his firewood in the bush on his own property behind the old house.

After taking all he could from his own land, he took to scouring the wasteland back of the dump road for trees that had been killed by insect infestations or lightning strikes. The wood belonged to someone else but the father had persuaded himself that it was a crime against man and nature to let potential fuel rot unused in the bush. In any case, he had no intention of letting his family freeze to death. He also knew that since the village garbage truck was the only vehicle to use the road in winter, there was little chance anyone would see him scrounging around on the private property in the vicinity. Even if the owner were to find out and complain to the police, the father was prepared to take his chances. He could expect little pity from the Provincial Police should they be called in, but should it be Old Jack who was entrusted with the case, there was little risk of sanction. The genial village constable was a good friend and often came to the old house for dinner on Sundays, particularly when baked beans were on the menu. He could be counted on to point out that only trees of no commercial value were being taken, and to do his best to smooth matters over.

The boy thus started to go with his father as he foraged for firewood. Accompanied by their malamute huskies pulling a sleigh, they would venture forth early Sunday mornings with axes and a crosscut saw with huge gaping teeth and proceed up the dump road past the place where the family had lived in a tent during their first summer in the village. They would then leave the road and range over the land until they found a dead tree. With his experience in the lumber camps, the father was an expert woodsman and a master with a crosscut saw. He would take one end of the family saw, and the boy the other. The boy lacked the strength to do anything other than hold the giant saw level as his father did the heavy work, pulling and pushing it through the wood. Then with the tree on the ground, the boy, taught by his father to handle a trimming axe, would do his share in removing the branches. Taking hold of the crosscut saw once again, the two would cut the trunk into manageable lengths.

When the snow was wet and deep, when the wind whipped and stung his face with ice pellets, it was misery. With the father in the lead, they would force themselves through heavy snow up to the boy's hips. The youngster's rubber boots, open at the top, would fill with snow that would turn to water on contact with his feet and then grow cold. But when there was a strong crust, when it was so cold there was not a cloud in the sky, when the hoarfrost on the trees sparkled and the smoke from chimneys throughout the village rose straight up to disappear into an azure sky, the work was easy and even fun. The boy would run and play with the dogs on rough land transformed into a level playing field. Then, aided by their dogs, father and son would drag their loads home on the sleigh, returning time and again until all the wood was safely stored in their backyard.

Every evening after school in the ensuing week, the boy would manoeuvre the rough logs up onto a sawhorse and use a small bucksaw to cut them into stove lengths, afterwards splitting the larger pieces into sizes to fit the firebox. Then, after carrying in armloads of wood to fill the box beside the stove, he would return to sit outside, oblivious to the state of the weather. Alone except for the reassuring company of the malamute huskies, he would think over the events of the day, enjoying his thoughts and cherishing the silence of the village in winter. Sometimes, if he was lucky, the night sky would erupt with the breathtaking spectacle of the Northern Lights shimmering and crackling above the mist rising from the fast-moving waters of the Indian River. Other times, he would sit quietly in gently falling snow and watch mesmerized as giant snowflakes drifted soundlessly through the light of street lamps in front of his home to blanket the silent highway – disturbed only infrequently at that time of the day and year by passing cars and trucks. He would, he thought, never find greater peace no matter how long he lived – and he was right.

The struggle to find wood to heat the old house would start again the following weekend.

By mid-March, it was the beginning of the spring thaw and the sounds, sights, tastes, and smells of the melt were in the air. The daytime temperatures rose, the hours of daylight lengthened, the snowbanks shrank, and the black asphalt of the highway was once again visible. The giant icicles hanging from the eaves of the old house softened, dripped furiously, and came crashing down, and the sodden, greasy snow on the roof slipped off with a whisper. In the soft, humid heat of the day, water droplets formed within the heavy snowpack on the hillsides, coalescing and percolating down to puddle on the ground, to seep out onto the shoulders of the highway and from there to run ever downwards to disappear into the Indian River.

At night, when the temperatures fell, a crust developed over the waterlogged snow, and ice formed on the meltwater. In the mornings, walking to school in the knee-high rubber boots he wore fall, winter, and spring, he was a boy of six again, scrambling over the rock-hard snowbanks to run on the crust and returning to jump from frozen puddle to frozen puddle, smashing and shattering into crystalline shards their coverings of semi-transparent wrinkled panes of ice. At recess, a sister skipped rope with her friends, chanting rhymes passed down from one generation of schoolgirls to the next over the years.

I like coffee, I like tea,
I like sitting on Bobby's knee.
Salute to the king and bow to the queen,
And turn your back on the gypsy queen!

In another part of the schoolyard, the boy played marbles with his brother and the other children, taking his turn tossing cat's eyes, rooster tails, plum shooters, and green streamers into a mound of moist sand piled up against the school wall. The one who succeeded in placing his marble closest to the wall won the jackpot. The boy lost some but won more, and usually returned to the classroom happy, his hands raw and cold, his nose running, his fingernails dirty, and his pockets filled with sand-covered booty of many colours.

After school, he splashed his way home through the streams of surface runoff water – a unique combination of melting snow, sand, gravel, crushed rock, dust, bark, twigs, dead leaves, and the acid rain pollution from distant smokestacks that together left an unforgettable metallic smell and aftertaste in nose and mouth. And like generations of village children before him at the time of the thaw, he stopped from time to time to play – absent-mindedly and drowsily shoving sand and dirt into the rivulets with his foot to create new channels, and building mini-dams to create mini-lakes and to hold back the flood – however temporarily.

On weekends, he carried out bologna sandwiches and soup to join the other members of his family on the back stoop to eat lunch in the fresh sunlit air. Afterwards, with the malamute huskies dancing alongside, excited at being freed from their chains to run loose through the melting, granular honey-combed snow of the bush, he tagged along as his father, his work shirt loosened and his pipe clenched between his teeth, crunched his way up the hill behind the old house. There, on a rocky, south-facing slope bare of snow, father and son sat in the sunny warmth radiating off the black, granite bedrock and listened to the cries of the crows and seagulls who reappeared over the Indian River every year at this time.

One day, seeking to preserve in his memory this special time in his life, the boy climbed on top of a snowdrift lying in the shade against the back of the old house and carved his initials and the date into the outside wall. And when the old house was being torn down forty years later, he returned to remove the board and carry it away.

As March turned to April, the snow vanished from the bush everywhere except in hemlock and cedar swamps so dense the sun never reached the ground, fishermen hauled their fish huts home, and the ice on the lakes disappeared. It was now the time of the "in-between" – between the departure of the snow and the arrival of the first leaves of the season. It was a time of sadness and a time of joy. On rainy days when black clouds hung low in the sky, black crows perched on black branches protruding from black tree trunks and sat on black fence posts. Icy rain mixed with snow beat down on withered dead leaves. Spectral pine trees clung to rock faces, their branches wrenched backwards behind their trunks into tortured arms by bitterly cold prevailing winds blowing from the west off the Georgian Bay. Pitiful specimens of cattle released from their winter confinement in low-ceilinged, filthy stables, their heads slumping, stood abjectly up to their knees in steaming wet manure outside dilapidated barns behind mean farmhouses smelling of poverty. And along the sides of the highway leading to the nearby town, the winter litter of empty cigarette packages, scraps of old newspapers, and empty beer bottles was only partially hidden by matted, wet, lifeless grass, and grit blown off the roadway from the winter sanding.

On days when the sun shone, however, red-winged blackbirds carried grass and twigs to build their nests in meadows inundated by the melting snow and in flooded marshes on pussy willow branches, which were themselves pushing out soft, silvery, and velvety buds. The pale-greens, lemon-yellows, and red-ochres of new-growth branches and twigs gave colour and life and vigour to the bush while pairs of broad-winged hawks, almost invisible against the blue sky with their white throats and light reddish chests, hunted mice, frogs, snakes, and insects in fields returning to life.

The wind-lashed pines on clifftops overlooking Lake Muskoka now assumed heroic poses – as if preparing themselves to be painted by one of the Group of Seven. The creeks swelled and burst their banks, the fish moved upriver to spawn, and frogs emerged from hibernation to lay their eggs and to sing. The dead grass, as it dried, changed from black to dark brown and then to tan. In backyards throughout the village, boys lit grass fires to give, so they said, the new shoots a better chance to grow. Summer residents who had not been to the village since Thanksgiving weekend the previous fall drove up from the big cities as they did at this time every year to inspect their properties, to hire local tradespeople to put their cottages in order, and to kickstart the local economy.

And an aging cousin of the boy's mother from the distant reserve, who had lost a leg in the war and who was spending the spring at his shack down at the Indian Camp, trapping muskrat and beaver, pushed his canoe out into the Indian River torrent. And whooping out a cry of delight in Chippewa, he rode it like a bucking horse through the floodwaters pouring over the stop logs in the dam, just as he did every year at this time, daring the gods of the river to do their worst.

And as they did at this time every year, the boy and his brother drilled holes in the sugar maples around the old house, inserted spigots, and hung tin cans to collect the sap. In the afternoons they gathered it in buckets and carried it inside to pour into shallow pans on the kitchen stove. They then stuffed the firebox with dry hardwood, stoked the fire into a blaze, and watched as the watery extract, bubbling furiously in a sea of white foam, and casting off thick clouds of steam, was reduced to a thick, smoky elixir. Afterwards, the happy family feasted on pancakes covered with maple syrup, and on maple toffee they made by boiling the liquid into a concentrated essence and pouring it still hot onto fresh clean snow to harden into chewy candy. And at night, in their overheated bedrooms filled with the humid, sweet smell of boiled sap, the family tossed and turned in their beds before falling asleep and dreaming of spring.

By May, when the leaves, wildflowers, leeks, watercress, and blackflies made their appearance, the father had forgotten his son's transgressions of the previous summer. And when July came, the boy stayed away from Big John at Whiting's Drugstore and Ice Cream Parlour.

ELEVEN

A Time of Transition

THE SUMMER OF 1952 WAS a time of transition for the village and for the boy. Fewer of the steamboats, whose arrival twice a day had been a feature of village life for decades, now docked at the government wharfs. The last survivors of the grand hotels, where formally attired guests dined on English bone china with silver cutlery and danced to the music of the big bands late into the night, went bankrupt or burned to the ground. The era when the district was the private playground of the very rich was over. But increasing numbers of Canada's growing middle class were discovering Muskoka, turning the shorelines into suburbia with their cottages, converting the waterways into boat-racing courses, and jamming the streets of the village with shoppers. Summer residents, who previously came only periodically to Port Carling between Labour Day and the May Victoria Day weekend, began winterizing their cottages and retiring in the village, in the process bringing in fresh ideas, changing old attitudes, and improving the quality of life. They would eventually even change the village from dry to wet.

Native people were now rarely to be seen on the benches around the docks in the evenings. The older generation was dying off, while the incoming one was finding work closer to home in the booming Canadian economy. Sulphuric acid blown from industrial smokestacks hundreds and even thousands of miles away came down in poisonous acid rain into the lakes to leach the mercury from the granite rock bottoms and enter the food chain. The lake trout, their flesh toxic, were wanted neither by the native fishermen for their families nor by their traditional customers. The cabins at the Indian Camp, with their pull-down counters displaying beadwork and quill baskets for sale, fell into ruin and were abandoned. Before long, the canoes along the shore would disappear. Soon only the giant white pines and a campsite for overnight visitors from the now prospering distant reserve would remain.

Visits from the mother's relatives for meals, a glass of raisin wine, and an evening of storytelling became rare. The boy missed them and was happy when his uncles from the reserve came looking for work in the village that summer. Both found employment but neither stayed long. The younger one, whom the boy had first met seven years earlier when he was a child at the Indian Camp, was now a heavy drinker and soon quit his job. The other, who had inherited his father's powerful physique, was a cheerful, hardworking brawler who had gained notoriety back on the reserve for picking up and heaving the Indian agent down the stairs of the community hall. Sharing the same bedroom as his young nephews, he kept them laughing with his earthy humour. He eventually threw a punch at his foreman and was fired. The boy's mother, afraid of the bad influence they could have on her boys, was relieved when her brothers moved on.

"You are welcome here any time, but only as long as you are sober and remain out of trouble."

Her brothers, who looked upon their older sister as a surrogate mother, never returned to stay. Rather, they telephoned her regularly to talk in Chippewa, to share their latest news, and to obtain her advice.

In the meantime, like everyone else in the village, the boy and his brother spent much of their spare time listening to the radio. In addition to *Fibber McGee and Molly*, their favourite programs were *The Shadow*, *Our Miss Brooks*, *The Lone Ranger*, and *The Green Hornet*. And late at night, when stations could be picked up from far away and when his brother was asleep, the boy would turn on the radio, keep the volume low, and listen to broadcasts from stations across the border. Indiscriminate in his tastes, the boy tuned in to anything that could be pulled out of the crackling, static-filled atmosphere, listening to dispassionate news reporters in Washington, D.C. outlining the latest developments in Congress, laconic sports announcers in Brooklyn covering the Yankees playing the Dodgers at Ebbets Field, fiery preachers in Louisville, Kentucky, with desperation in their voices, urging listeners to repent or go to hell, and disc jockeys playing the records of gospel singers celebrating their faith, of jazz musicians being ever so cool, of rhythm and blues performers on the upbeat, and of country music artists breaking their hearts for the public.

The Grand Ole Opry, transmitted from Nashville, Tennessee, was one of his favourites. For the songs about poor, down-and-out country folk looking for work, drinking too much, failing or succeeding at love, having run-ins with the law, brawling, and wandering the soulless megacities of the land had a special appeal for him since they described the woes and joys of the life of the average guy. The big hits that summer were "I'll Never Get Out of This World Alive" by Hank Williams and "I Didn't Know God Made Honky Tonk Angels" by Hank Thomas.

Even the frantic hucksters flogging all manner of

quack medical remedies, miracle formulas to improve the performance of automobile engines, brake pads and windshield wipers, cigarettes and chewing tobacco that were "healthy, wholesome, and guaranteed to get you a girl," and nostrums to grow hair on bald heads pledging "satisfaction or your money back" had their appeal. No matter how remote the experiences were to the life he knew in his small village or how outlandish the claims, the radio spoke to him directly and personally, letting him know that a world out there beyond Muskoka existed, to be explored, enjoyed, and lived.

But the radio era was ending, and the television age was beginning. Already a merchant had opened a store selling television sets. A crowd of the curious congregated every night on the street outside his showroom and watched *I Love Lucy*, *Arthur Godfrey*, and *Dragnet*. The sound was largely inaudible through the plate glass windows. Pulled from the airwaves with the help of a giant antenna from stations in distant Toronto and Buffalo, the images were always snowy. But no one cared. Everyone was enthralled by the mystery of moving pictures broadcast from somewhere far away and appearing as if by magic on a screen before their eyes. Soon most villagers would own television sets.

The boy was one of the most faithful members of the crowd standing outside the showroom window. He was there not because he particularly liked the programs. He actually preferred the shows, dramas, news, and even the hockey games broadcast on the radio, since they left more to the imagination. Nor was he especially interested in the high technology on display. Rather, the flickering images he saw through the glass reminded him of a problem he understood only vaguely and that from time to time preoccupied him.

Every so often, while going about the routine business of his day, whether immersed in his homework, doing his chores, or talking to his best friend, he would suddenly feel surprise bordering on astonishment that he even existed. The objects around him, no matter how mundane – a piece of birchbark, a block of firewood, the oilcloth on the kitchen table, a buzzing fly, a spider spinning its web, the torn cover of a book – would suddenly become infused with an unexpected and often beautiful vitality. It was as if another being had taken possession of his body and was watching him interact with a world that had an existence of its own. The flashes of awareness and wonder at the miracle of life would soon pass, and he would return to the routine of everyday reality. With the passage of time, the sparks of intuition would come less and less often, until they appeared only when he was sitting alone, listening to inspiring music or reading poetry.

At this time of his life, however, when he was no

longer a child but not yet an adolescent, he would puzzle over what was happening and why. It was not the sort of issue he could discuss with the other guys, with his parents or with a teacher, for fear that they would think he was odd. Not sure anyone else had similar experiences, he tried to think the problem through on his own. That gave rise, however, to other questions. Why had he received the gift of existence? Who was he anyhow? What was the purpose of life? As he watched the rudimentary television images on the main street of Port Carling, he thought perhaps he was just playing a part in a cosmic television play. This answer, however unlikely, seemed just as valid as any other.

A series of deaths in the village that summer then raised issues of a more sombre nature. A prosperous neighbour, who had purchased a television set and wanted to do a good deed, made welcome a five-year-old from a poor family to watch a children's program. When the program was over, the youngster ran down the centre of the street on his way home and was hit by a car and killed. The boy was perplexed. He asked himself how it was possible that generosity could lead to the death of a child? He also had to rethink his assumptions about the cycle of life. He had taken for granted that one was born, passed from childhood to boyhood, to adolescence, to maturity, to old age and finally to death.

The town clerk, for example, who four years earlier had relentlessly pressed the boy's mother to pay her property tax arrears or face the forced sale of her home, died peacefully in his sleep. The turnout at his funeral service was impressive. Much was made in the eulogies about his outstanding life and the contribution he had made to his community for so many years. No one mentioned his ruthless tax-collection methods. To the mournful tolling of the bells from the Presbyterian church, a throng accompanied his coffin to the cemetery. That was the way it was supposed to be, the boy thought. He was an old man and his time had come.

But it was different with the little boy, whose life had been snuffed out as he ran joyously home, his head filled with the marvels of the just-viewed television images. Although the boy had stopped going to church by this time, he attended the funeral service as part of a contingent of student mourners assembled by the Anglican priest for the occasion. He viewed the tiny body in the open coffin and heard the cleric try to explain in religious terms why innocent children had to die. From the look of anguish in his eyes, the priest himself, the boy suspected, found it hard to believe his own explanations.

The father of the child, a much-battered, unemployed former professional boxer, an alcoholic and a sometime poet from the big city who had married a local girl, entered the church. Wearing an old and tattered suit jacket over a tie-less shirt, his pallid, broken face swollen from crying, he held tightly to his grief-stricken wife in a heart-rending scene the boy would never forget. After the service, the father told the press he had been travelling on a bus from Toronto to Port Carling when his son was killed. At the instant of the child's death, the father had a premonition his son was dead. He was still struggling to come to terms with the tragedy, but was confident the meaning of his death would be revealed in the fullness of time.

But the boy did not believe him. Nor would he ever understand how someone who had shown no pity to his mother when she was in such great need, and probably to other poor people as well, could live to a ripe old age while an innocent child should die before he had started to live.

Then in August, it rained non-stop throughout one weekend. Cottagers and tourists stayed away from the village, and the locals remained indoors. On the Monday morning, a high school student who had a summer job working in a souvenir shop above Whiting's Drug Store and Ice Cream Parlour, found his employer slumped over, dead, his body in a chair and his head resting on the railing overlooking the docks. Empty whisky and sleeping-pill bottles were by his side. He had died just above the dockside bench where the boy had spent so many happy hours reading comic books and eating ice cream cones just two years earlier. The villagers said he could not take the loneliness and the rain. The boy believed that the stranger had killed himself to escape the same sort of depression that returned periodically to torment his mother.

The boy's family would soon be able to install an indoor toilet and shower in the old house. Within two or three years, they would even be able to purchase a television set despite the high cost. For the family's economic fortunes were improving. The boy's father had found steady employment working on the estate of a wealthy American in the summers and picking up odd jobs in the winter. And in the development that would lift the family forever out of poverty, the mother went out to work.

The man who set this happy train of events in progress was an old Jewish friend of her father who had often dropped in to chat or buy lake trout from him at his home at the Indian Camp during the Great Depression. Later, he had opened a small tourist lodge in the village to cater to Jews who were made to feel unwelcome or simply turned away in that era of open anti-Semitism from the mainstream tourist hotels in the area. Now he stopped the boy's mother in the street.

"I'm having trouble finding good help at the lodge. Why don't you come and see if the work suits you? And bring your kids. They can play with the children of the guests on the beach and eat with the rest of us in the staff dining room. The food is kosher, but I guarantee they'll like it."

The boy's mother soon reported for work, discovering that it helped relieve her depression as well as bring in a second income.

As for the boy, it was his first contact with Jews. He had, however, often heard his parents talk of a Jewish doctor who had saved his brother's life the year before the family moved to Port Carling. His brother, sick with pneumonia, had been given up for lost, and his mother had been summoned to the hospital to be with him as he died. The doctor, however, managed to obtain a small supply of penicillin, the miracle drug that had just been developed and reserved for use on wounded soldiers in Europe. Instead of dying, his brother pulled through and the parents credited the fact that the doctor came from a community of people renowned for their great learning for saving his life. The boy was familiar with the stories of the Jewish people in the Bible from his Sunday school classes. He had also heard the usual racist remarks about them in the schoolyard. Exposed to the real people, however, he found the friendly proprietor, his family, and the middle-class Jewish vacationers no different from anyone else.

This applied to the young, good-natured waiters from the big city who laughed and joked in the dining room.

Until the day the boy saw the numbers tattooed on their arms. The young men were different, he saw, not because they were Jews, but because of the terrible things they had suffered. They were Holocaust survivors, refugees to Canada who were given summer work by the tourist lodge owner. The boy knew something of what they had been through since his uncle had been a war photographer in the Canadian Army who had entered the death camps in 1945 and afterwards tried to relate to his family the horrible things he had seen.

From their experiences, the boy believed, the waiters had gained insights into the joy of living and the tragedy of death that set them apart from anyone he knew or would ever know. He wanted to ask them about the questions that perplexed him, but sensing they would not want to talk about anything that reminded them of their sufferings, said nothing. In later life, however, whenever he faced problems that seemed insurmountable, he would think of the young men he met that summer, who had endured such pain and yet retained such a passion for life.

TWELVE

—

Blood Sports

WHEN HER JOB ENDED AT the Jewish lodge, the mother accepted employment from a growing number of summer residents as a cleaning lady. For his part, the boy was now able to make his own modest contribution to the family finances, giving half of his earnings from all sources to his mother, starting with those from his paper route, as had been his original plan. Like the other boys in the village of his age, while not paid much, he found sporadic employment on weekends in the spring raking leaves, painting porches, and carrying out the myriad of tasks needed to prepare cottages for occupancy. In the summers, he worked part-time at Hanna's General Store, stocking shelves and bagging groceries. He was hired from time to time by local contractors helping out with maintenance work at the homes of summer residents, washing windows, cutting grass and firewood, and in his spare time, he caddied at the nearby Muskoka Lakes Golf and Country Club. In the winters, he shovelled snow off roofs. He also began to make a tidy sum collecting empty pop and beer bottles spring, summer, and fall, and redeeming them for two cents each.

If he had really wanted, he could have earned much more. An elderly stranger came to the village with a supply of cash and an ambition to make his fortune in real estate as fast as possible, even if he had to cut a few legal corners to do so. In short order he bought a block of land located on the other side of the road behind a dozen high-end cottages on one of the most desirable local lakes, as well as an old cottage on the Indian River close to the boy's home. His intention, which he shamelessly made known to anyone who would listen, was to subdivide his land into lots and find some way to force the nearby wealthy summer residents to buy them at exorbitant prices. Meanwhile he would live in the old cottage until he found some way to offload it at an inflated price to some unsuspecting tourist.

The summer residents had no interest in buying the lots behind their cottages since none of them fronted on the lake. The old rascal knew this, of course. So he rented a truck and started hauling garbage and derelict cars out to his property, telling his intended victims that he would turn his holdings into a dumpsite if they did not buy him out. In short order, they yielded to his blackmail, and the stranger pocketed a quick and easy profit.

Having made his money – and made himself unwelcome in the village as a result of his shady dealings – the stranger wanted to get rid of his cottage as soon as possible and move on. But how could he make a fast dollar on it? He devised a plan, but needed partners in crime. But where could he find collaborators in a small, law-abiding village? The boy and his brother were the obvious candidates. As aboriginals living in a ramshackle old house, they were obviously good criminal material. He invited them to come see him and made a "business" proposal.

Would they burn down his cottage? He had insured it for much more than it was worth, and wanted to cash in. He proposed establishing a good alibi for himself by returning to visit his family for a day or two in the distant city from whence he came. In his absence, they could do the deed and in return he would pay them handsomely after the insurance company settled his claim.

The boy maliciously played along.

"And how much would be our share?"

As his brother looked on smiling, he then raised the expectations of the old scoundrel by pretending interest and bargaining hard for a higher payoff. After squeezing out a higher offer, he dashed the crook's hopes by telling him to find someone else to do his dirty work. The disappointed stranger then abandoned his scheme, eventually selling his cottage for as much as he could get for it legitimately and leaving the village.

The boy thought no more of the matter, for by that time he had decided to go into the scrap metal business. It had all started with a conversation he had with his Scottish grandfather. He was a fierce defender of the rights of workers and the common man and was opposed to all conflicts, including the Korean War, as a matter of principle.

"Do you realize, laddie, the capitalists are constantly fighting among themselves and want wars because conflicts make them even richer! For them it's just a blood sport. It's a shameful thing. Metal is needed to make weapons to fuel the war machine in Korea and prices have skyrocketed! Today, as we speak, there are profiteers making a killing selling scrap copper, lead, and zinc!"

The boy listened carefully to the wise words of his grandfather. He shared his political sentiments, or at least he thought he did. But if prices had skyrocketed, just think of the money he could make selling scrap metal! And he knew exactly where to find it. He headed for the dump.

But the boy quickly learned that the competition among capitalists to corner the scrap metal supplies at the Port Carling dump was ferocious. He had been delighted to find abundant supplies of old copper wiring discarded by electricians and damaged lead and zinc pipes thrown out by plumbers. But as he was pulling his treasures from the trash, the woman who owned the property around the dump came out of the bush, shaking her fist and spitting.

"You git outta here! That scrap is mine. If I ever see you around here agin, I'll kick your bum right up to your shoulders!"

The boy withdrew grudgingly and empty-handed. He did not want to abandon his acquisitions but knew she meant business. Although getting on in years, the woman, tall, lean, and broad-shouldered, was exceptionally powerful, and capable of giving a good hiding to most of the men of the village, not to mention a twelve-year-old kid.

A second-generation descendant of an old pioneer family, she operated a hard-scrabble pig and dairy farm within the village limits. The sight of her animals grazing in the rough pasture carved out of a swamp in front of her farmhouse was an accepted part of village life, and no one complained about the occasional whiff of pig manure that drifted over the village from her barn. In fact, her pigs had become something of a tourist attraction. So inbred were her boars and sows, their offspring more often than not were hermaphrodite – sporting male and female sexual organs on the same body.

The word *hermaphrodite* being a big one, the locals as often as not described them as "them thar haemorrhoid pigs over at the old farm," but everyone knew what they meant. Visitors from the big cities in the south made side trips to the village to see them. And in response to requests for directions to see the unusual pigs, village wits would respond that "there's piles and piles of them at the old farm leading out of town" and laugh uproariously, pleased at the subtlety of their secret joke.

Unfortunately, the woman's pigs and cattle often broke through the poorly maintained fencing around her property and roamed the village at will. To make matters worse, her animals were not Disney World kind-and-gentle Clarabelle Cows and loveable Porky Pigs. They were mud- and manure-covered rampaging sows, boars, cows, steers, and bulls – gigantic, organic throwbacks to the original stock of the pioneers, with wicked eyes and attitudes to match. Boars and sows alike resembled miniature hippopotamuses; with tusks curling out of their mouths, and teats and testicles on high alert, they would charge anyone foolish enough to try to shoo them away. As for the errant cattle, they came equipped with racks of huge, sharply pointed horns, one side always longer than the other, Texas Longhorn style; they strutted rather than walked down the main street, tails snapping, daring anyone to take them on.

The village fathers, while appreciating that hermaphrodite pigs constituted a valuable tourist attraction, frowned on exposing summer visitors to close-up views of them wandering the streets. Times were changing, and they were anxious to cultivate a more genteel image of their community to attract a more sophisticated tourist trade. The woman's neighbours, for their part, did not appreciate pigs rooting in their potato, carrot, and beet beds, and running amok through their corn patches. Those with lawns were unhappy with the presence of cattle grazing in their front yards. Complaint after complaint was lodged with Old Jack. The woman, however, scoffed at their grievances and thumbed her nose at the fines the local authorities levied on her for letting her animals run wild.

The boy and his best friend, however, maintained good relations with her, and often dropped by her farm to pass the time of day, gossip, and joke. There was not a more fascinating place in the village for the boys to hang out. Where else could they witness free-ranging chickens wandering from the barnyard unhindered into an acrid, dung-bespattered dairy, defecating at will, and drinking their fill from milk being bottled for delivery to unsuspecting summer residents? Where else could they watch trucks laden with barrels of reeking swill from the kitchens of tourist resorts roll in to be slopped to snorting, groaning, grunting stinking swine? Where else could they obtain privileged close-up views of the giant hermaphrodite pigs and their intriguing sexual organs? And where better to admire the feats of strength of the strongest woman in the village as she heaved heavy bags of pig feed around like feather pillows? She, in turn, had always extended the boys a friendly, if rough-and-tough, welcome.

However, business was business and capitalism was capitalism. She was also in a bad mood and not disposed to be flexible after a recent incident that had made her the laughingstock of the village. Another old-timer, whose property abutted hers, had shot one of her bulls carefully between the eyes with his .303 hunting rifle. It had been grazing in his front yard, and he wanted to send a message to his neighbour to keep her animals at home. The woman summoned Old Jack, who decreed that it was illegal to shoot someone's livestock even if said livestock was eating one's flowers and leaving enormous quantities of unwanted fresh fertilizer on one's lawn. He issued a summons for the old-timer to appear in court.

The scene was thus set for a confrontation between the ageing offspring of the pioneers. Unlike the characters of *High Noon*, the award-winning film then playing in the movie theatre of the nearby town where a hero faced off against a set of villains, there were no good guys in this showdown, for the old-timer was no Gary Cooper. He had been notorious for years in the village for his anti-social antics and his hateful opinions. With a floppy felt hat on his head, corncob pipe clenched in his yellow teeth, and with one brace holding up his raggedy overalls, he could be counted on to provide to anyone who would listen his unvarnished and ignorant views on the perils of modernity, the inferiority of women, the vanity of his wife, who had dared to put curtains on the windows of their house, the nefarious influence of rich tourists who were ruining the pioneer legacy of the community, the evil influence of "furriners" who were undermining the Canada he had known in his youth, and the lazy Indians, who spent their summers "up to no good" down at the Indian Camp. He was also the village drunk, and his mishaps had become the source of local folklore. The villagers were still talking about an incident the previous winter when he fell asleep on the side of the road during an evening snowstorm and was scooped up by a snowplough and deposited unhurt in a snowbank, where he slept contentedly until dawn.

Everyone recognized his faults, but he had blood ties to more than half of the people in the village, who felt obliged to defend him on the grounds he was family. The other half, with the exception of the boy and his family, who winced whenever they heard him rant on about Indians, tolerated his excesses and looked upon his actions and words as harmless. Some even said he was so colourful, he had become an attraction as valuable as "them thar haemorrhoid pigs" in drawing tourists to the village. The only time his antics outraged everyone was when he called a distinguished Jewish war veteran from the big city "a dirty Nazi." The Legion members expelled him from their ranks. In revenge, he took to getting drunk, covering his face with his old felt hat, and sleeping off his binges on the lawn in front of the Legion hall.

On the day of the trial, the woman travelled to the nearby town to testify against her neighbour. She demanded and expected justice. But to her chagrin, a convoy of villagers took a day off work and travelled in their pickup trucks and cars to the courthouse to show support for the shooter and not for her. At the trial itself, the old-timer was fortunate to find himself up before a judge who preferred making jokes that would amuse the crowd to dispensing justice. He observed that it was the first time in almost fifty years on the bench that someone had been hauled up before him for "shooting the bull." He laughed so hard, and his sally was so well received by the villagers and by the usual loafers hanging out in his courtroom, that he levied the minimum fine and let the offender go.

By trivializing and making fun of the case against the village drunk, the judge humiliated the woman. Now, clearly, she was in no mood to tolerate the competition that came so soon afterwards from the young whipper-snapper seeking to help himself to what she had come to believe was her personal scrap metal preserve at the dump.

But the next morning, at a time so early even the sun and farmers were not up, the boy woke up with a start in the bed he shared with his brother. So intent was he on returning to the site of their confrontation and retrieving his scrap metal, he had needed no alarm clock to tell him it was time to rise. Everyone else in the house was asleep, which was the way he wanted it to be.

As the youngster slipped out of bed, he had a momentary fright as his brother muttered to himself and shifted his position – but carried on sleeping. Picking up his shoes and gathering together his pants, shirt and socks from the floor where he had tossed them before crawling into bed the night before, the boy crept down the stairs. After quickly dressing, he stuck his head under the faucet and drank his fill of ice-cold water. Pushing open the screen door, he tiptoed across the porch and stood facing the highway. The air at this time before sunrise was cool and humid and a sliver of moon was still visible in the brightening Eastern sky. Off in the distance, invisible birds were starting to call to each other and the smell of decaying vegetation and the occasional deep croak of a bullfrog came from the direction of the creek that ran into the Indian River, a stone's throw away at the bottom of the hill. On a small knoll close to the house, the malamute huskies, attached by long chains to their kennels, greeted him with low-pitched friendly yelps. They seemed to sense he wanted no one in the house to know he was up and outdoors, and kept their greetings discreet. The boy, as he always did when leaving the house, went first to the dogs to murmur an affectionate hello, to embrace them and to scratch their ears.

Then taking a shortcut off the path and up the hill, soaking his pants to the hips in the process, he waded through tall dew-drenched grass to the highway and was soon on the side road leading to the dump. His days of play-acting and hunting imaginary Nazis long over, he was a boy on a mission to reclaim what rightfully belonged to him. As expected, he met no one.

The three families who had lived on the dump road in the summer of 1946 had moved on and abandoned their houses. Their dark silhouettes, deserted and silent, loomed against the lightening sky as he hurried past them. One, a burned-out shell, had been torched by arsonists some months earlier and the smell of charred, damp wood still hung in the air. The boy wondered if the old stranger who had sought to recruit him to burn down his cottage was in some way implicated.

The deserted road was transformed into a long black tunnel by the overarching branches of the trees along its sides. The boy was nervous and on edge, afraid that wild animals, or worse, the woman who had chased him from the dump, were lying in wait for him in the shadows. But he was so angry at her and so consumed with humiliation and self-righteous indignation at the injustice of it all that he soon forgot his fears, and before he knew it, was at the dump. As expected, his scrap metal was no longer where he had left it. He could see it, however, in plain view in the milky-grey predawn light in a clearing on the other side of the rundown barbed wire fence that marked the woman's property line.

"She thinks I'll be afraid to touch it. She can't scare me. I'll show her!"

The boy removed his scrap metal and took it home. Thereafter he confined his foraging trips to the dump to the earliest hours of the morning. He also spread the word of his new business interests to his newspaper customers, who started saving scrap metal for him. The owner of an old hotel told him to take what he wanted from a pile of lead and copper pipes that had been lying in the tall grass behind the building for years. Soon the boy branched out and began to collect scrap iron and steel as well. The village doctor gave him a damaged metal operating-room table. Villagers began dropping off at his home old metal bedsteads and worn-out cast-iron stoves. A mound of scrap metal took form in his backyard.

When it was time, the boy went to see his parents.

"If you hire a truck and driver for me to take the metal to a scrap yard, I'll split the profits with you."

The scrap merchant in the distant town paid him eighty dollars. He paid the driver twenty dollars and he and his parents shared the other sixty. Capitalism, even the tooth and claw variety, he discovered, brought handsome rewards, even if he was no longer welcome at his competitor's farm.

With his share of his scrap metal earnings and other savings, the boy set out to buy an up-to-date shotgun. He was now old enough, he told himself, to move from hunting small game and go after deer like the big guys and men. His best friend had already shot his first deer, and the boy wanted to prove himself as well. To do so, however, he would have to put aside his .22 rifle, too light for his new purpose, and the ancient ten-gauge monster that he had never been able to master. After consulting the advertisements in the *Family Herald*, he sent away for a Winchester repeating shotgun.

> *Tiny WP stamped on the barrel from Olin Industries, Inc., New Haven 4, Conn. Metal parts are "machined" from Winchester Proof chrome-molybdenum Steel. The Natural Pointer. Genuine American Walnut stock and slide handle, richly finished. Fool-proof cross bolt trigger lock. Shells chamber perfectly, eject easily.*

His father disapproved. "Life is sacred, my boy, and we humans are animals too. And the days when our family needed game for food are over."

The father's advice came at a time when he had started to pay more attention to the boy and his brother. Their formal education he ignored, and he was indifferent to whether or not they did well in school. Yet now that his boys were almost the age he had reached when he left home to make his way in the world, he wanted to pass on to them his values and the meaning of life as he understood it. Not one to set limits, he wanted his boys to learn from his example.

Just to be certain they did not think he was becoming sentimental, however, he repeated to them a little private joke.

"My boys, I want you to know that I have always regretted raising kids instead of pigs. Both are messy, but with pigs I could have made a bit of money with a lot less bother."

And then, with a laugh, he took them on hiking and berry-picking trips on the trails back of the dump to reinforce his conviction that life in all its forms was sacrosanct. He identified for them white-throated sparrows, belted kingfishers, sandpipers, and pileated woodpeckers. When they encountered snakes, he stopped his sons from killing them on sight, as had been their practice, and picked them up to show they were inoffensive and beautiful in their own way. When they saw rabbits, squirrels, foxes, and partridges, he wondered aloud what pleasure anyone could obtain by killing such attractive creatures endowed with such life force.

In the spring, he exposed them to the beauty of the wildflowers that carpeted the bush floor at that time of the year, drawing attention in particular to his favourites – trilliums, jack-in-the-pulpits, touch-me-nots, lady's slippers, dog tooth violets, and bluebells. Wildflowers, he told them, were not to be picked. Wild leeks, with their powerful onion and garlic smell, and watercress with its pungent petals, traditional spring foods of the native people and early settlers, were another matter, and he pointed out to his boys where, when, and how to gather them. In excursions that summer, he took his sons on blueberry-picking expeditions and identified for them Queen Anne's lace, daisies in all their varieties, orange hawkweeds, black-eyed Susans, and buttercups as well as the bullhead lilies, white water lilies, and cattails in the mud lakes and swamps. The orange hawkweeds, trilliums, and bullhead lilies would remain the boy's lifelong favourites.

He also took them around the big lakes in a second-hand Dippie, purchased for ten dollars, to point out navigation hazards and show them the best angling places, just in case they decided to make fishing their life vocation. The father's Dippie was a heavy, much-patched dinosaur with a worn-out engine that failed at least once every time it was taken out. The boys eventually grew tired of rowing the leaky old tub home and started to make excuses to avoid further trips to the outer reaches of the Muskoka Lakes.

Even though the brothers learned more from their father that spring and summer than at any other time in their lives, they were also of an age when they thought they knew it all. For the father's attention to them came just as they were readying themselves to break free of parental constraints. The boy's brother, now almost fifteen, was looking forward to leaving school and getting a job, and in fact would do so within the year. The boy had ambitions that involved remaining in school and staying at home for a few more years to do so, but he had not discussed them with his parents, and was uncertain whether his dreams were mere fantasies of the type he had indulged in when he was younger. Thus while the boy listened to his father's words about his gun purchase, he paid him no heed.

The boy's mother said nothing about his hunting plans, but he believed that she approved. Game was the traditional food of the native people and good hunters were highly regarded among the Chippewa. She had already praised the boy when he returned home in previous years with rabbits, partridge, and ducks.

Every weekend, starting in early October, the boy with his new shotgun loaded with number one shot for bringing down big game, and his best friend with his father's .303 hunting rifle, roamed the bush back of the dump. They now disdained the rabbits and partridge they had previously coveted. As the weeks passed, the leaves changed colour and fell from the trees. Soon frost lay on the ground when they went out early in the morning. Then in late October came the first snowfall. And with the first snow appeared the tracks of a deer.

The two set off in pursuit. The boy's heart was racing. He had heard many stories of first-time hunters becoming gun-shy and freezing when faced with shooting their first deer and letting the animal escape. They became the laughingstock of the hunting fraternity.

"What's a matter? Afraid of a little deer? Did you do it in your pants when you saw the deer?" And so on.

That would not happen to him.

The boys followed the tracks in the snow through swamps and over ridges. The deer frantically tried to outrun them, but the boys pressed on. Late in the day, many miles from where they started, the boy finally saw the deer, a mature stag with a huge rack of antlers standing and looking at him quietly from a short distance away.

He would not be gun-shy. He would not freeze. He would not be a laughingstock. He would shoot and become a man.

He raised his shotgun, aimed it hurriedly in the general direction of his prey, and pulled the trigger.

The stag leapt in the air and with two bounds was gone.

The boy felt sick. How could he have fired on such a magnificent living being. He was heartbroken when he saw the blood. He had hit the animal but not brought it down.

"Good shot! He can't be far!"

His best friend was triumphant.

The boy put on a brave face.

"Let's go get him. Can't be far."

The boys tracked the deer in vain until it grew dark. When he went home that night, the boy put away his shotgun and vowed never to hunt again – a promise to himself that he would not keep.

THIRTEEN

—

Coming of Age

IT WAS THE SUMMER OF 1953 and the boy was now a thirteen-year-old teenager. He thought mainly about sex. Not about girls, but about sex. Actually, all the guys in the village were thinking about sex. The older ones who had left school, and who could afford to buy beat-up old cars and pickup trucks, were doing more than just thinking about it. At the end of each workday they would rush home, hurriedly wash off the grime of the day, shave (whether they needed to or not), slather on aftershave lotion, grind sticks of deodorant against their armpits, don clean shirts, roll up the sleeves to expose their muscles, and gobble down their dinners. And then with sunburned arms nonchalantly dangling from the open windows of their cars and fresh stalks of timothy hay urbanely grasped between their front teeth, they would go cruising, two to a car, up and down the street running through the village.

Their targets were the chambermaids and waitresses spending their summers working at the tourist lodges and the big summer hotels on the surrounding lakes. They did not have to go far. The girls, from distant villages and towns with rich, picturesque names in Ontario's north like Sturgeon Falls, Capreol, South Porcupine, Iroquois Falls, Kapuskasing, and Hearst, were to be found in large numbers each evening hitchhiking through the village on their way to nowhere in particular and looking for some excitement to liven up the tedium of their lives. The happy locals were more than willing to do what they could to accommodate their desires.

The courting techniques of the village Don Juans were simple but effective. On sighting prospective victims, they would honk their horns and yell "Yee-haw" – the war cry of all proud, young Muskoka males – at the top of their lungs. This alerted the girls to their presence and warned off competitors – much in the way bull moose bellow to attract female moose and drive off other bull moose during the rutting season. They would then gun their motors and race their vehicles as fast as they could up the road, slamming on the brakes at just the right moment to come to a screeching, rubber-burning halt just beside the appreciative girls. Grinning broadly, they would then lean out their windows and engage in subtle small talk such as: "Hey thar good look'n, you wanna go fer a ride?" The girls invariably said yes.

The boy and the other guys his age, however, could only watch their older peers in action, admire the sophistication of their methods, and dream of the day when they too would be old enough to buy an old jalopy and join the annual summer chase. While waiting for that happy day, they spent their time ogling the ads for women's undergarments and bathing suits in Eaton's catalogue in that era before *Playboy* magazine appeared on the newsstands and, of course, they spent hours talking about sex. Their conversations were dominated by the raciest of jokes that usually started with "Didya hear the one about the salesman and the farmer's daughter?" And no matter how often they heard the same joke, they all laughed uproariously, nervous and self-conscious.

The boy was anxious to do more than look at lingerie ads and to talk about sex, but did not know any girls he could seduce. The girls in his class he excluded, for they were too much like sisters. The teenagers in the high school he lusted after, but they did not know he existed. Perhaps, he thought, he could find a girlfriend from outside the village. Leafing through the *Family Herald*, he came across the pen pal section.

Maude from Belle Island, Newfoundland, was seeking a soulmate. With the same insouciance he had displayed some years earlier in answering an advertisement from the same magazine to obtain the secrets of raising red hybrid earthworms, the boy wrote her a letter. He thought it prudent not to mention he was only thirteen.

Dear Maude,
I saw your name in the *Family Herald* looking for a pen pal. I am a student at the Port Carling Elementary and High School in Muskoka Ontario and would like to get to know you. Port Carling is the centre of Canada's tourist industry. Please write and send a picture.
Yours Truly,
Jimmy

Ten days later, a letter arrived from Maude.

Dear Jimmy,
Thank you so much for answering my request for a pen pal. I am 18 and in grade 9. My dad has the black lung from working in the coal mine. Theirs no work here. I want to cum to Ontario to live. Do you think I could find work in the tourist

industry? Can you help me? Can I cum see you?
Attached is my pickture.
Yours Truly,
Maude

The boy stared at the photograph of his new friend with some trepidation. Maude was a pleasant, plump, matronly looking lady about twice his size. She also appeared a lot older than eighteen. In fact, she looked older than his teacher. He wrote back.

Dear Maude,
Thank you for your letter. I'm really sorry about your dad.
We're moving. Please don't come.
Yours Truly,
Jimmy

He might, he admitted, be somewhat young to embark on a pen pal romance. He would take his chances locally. But first he would have to change his image. For when he looked in the mirror, a baby-faced, scrawny callow kid with tufts of hair shooting up uncontrollably in all directions stared back at him. Perhaps the solution was to turn himself into a "Brylcreem Man"? Or perhaps a "Brylcreem Teenager," if there was such a thing? After all, the advertisements on the barber shop wall proclaimed "A Little Dab'll Do Ya," and Brylcreem men always had beautiful women hanging on to their arms, their faces turned admiringly towards their slicked-down and shiny hair.

The boy bought a tube and applied a dab. His hair, however, clearly had not heard the commercial and refused to co-operate. The boy applied dab after dab until his hair was finally sleek and shiny and slicked down, just like the models in the advertisement. Now a baby-faced callow kid, with not even the hint of a beard, with slicked-down, greasy hair and looking no older than ten, returned his gaze when he admired himself in the mirror.

Then gradually the boy's vision blurred. Was he going blind? And was becoming blind part of the process of becoming a man? He had heard that if teenagers did certain unmentionable things to themselves in private, they could go blind! But to his relief he found it was just the dabs melting and leaking liquid Brylcreem down across his forehead and into his eyes.

Despite these setbacks, the boy still lived in hope, as did the other guys his age, that he might "get lucky." But what then? Like the other guys, he was torn between the desire to find a willing partner and the fear of actually having his wish come true. For, as all the guys "knew," it was all too easy to get a girl into trouble. And that, as the guys likewise "knew," was the worst thing that could possibly happen, because then you had to get married, even if you were only thirteen! In those days before the sexual revolution and the pro-choice movement, it was unheard of for girls or women to raise children without being married. The guys were also certain there were no unmarried mothers in Port Carling; for if there were, they would have been the first to know.

It was common knowledge, however, that there was an unmarried mother in the nearby town who was raising two children alone, supporting herself by working in a variety store. Her defiance of local morality constituted one of the great scandals of the district, and she was branded as a shameless degenerate. The boys would drop into the store, pretend to be interested in the merchandise for sale, and surreptitiously sneak looks at Muskoka's very own fallen woman. A true wanton woman, they figured, should wear a skin-tight sweater and a flimsy dress, her eyes should be framed by dark mascara, her lips should be smeared with a vulgar shade of lipstick, her cheeks should be plastered with offsetting white powder, her fingernails should be long and painted black, her entire body should be drenched in cheap French toilet water, and her voice should be low and sultry.

Unfortunately, the woman neither looked nor acted the part of a debauched, fast-living hussy. She was plain, somewhat dumpy and good-hearted, her clothes were practical, her face was ruddy and well-scrubbed, her fingernails were short and clean, and her laugh booming and friendly. In short, she was altogether most ordinary.

The boys, however, were self-appointed arbiters of morality as cynical in their own way as the most gossipy old busybodies. They explained away the discrepancy between image and reality by claiming the saleslady most likely led two lives – the respectable one on display by day, and one of private debauchery by night.

Closer to home, they were also convinced that everyone who got married in Port Carling "had to," except perhaps for the United Church, Anglican, and Presbyterian ministers – and even here they had their suspicions. When happy brides and grooms emerged from church to wave to friends and relatives before climbing into their cars and departing on their honeymoons, the boys would be ready with their off-colour commentary.

"When d'ya think the baby will be born? From the size of her, look's to me like it'll be in about five months. I bet it wasn't even his fault. We'll know who the father really is when we see the colour of the baby's hair." And on and on.

To avoid a similar fate, the boy and his friends agreed that you always had to use a condom. The other guys told the boy that their parents "did it" and had stocks stashed away to prevent "accidents." They had helped themselves to copious supplies from their parents' bedrooms and kept them at the ready in their wallets. The boy was ready to believe his friends' parents "did it" but surely not his own mother and father. They were his parents, for Pete's sake!

Just to be sure, however, he went into their bedroom to confirm his assumption and to disappointment mixed with relief found none. But lying innocently on the dresser was a book. On the cover was a banal portrait of a lady smiling primly and wearing a sunbonnet. To the boy, however, the portrait was a lurid picture of a sultry southern beauty inviting adventurous prospective readers to pick up the book. He grabbed it and left.

His brother, older and wiser in the ways of the world, gave him a condom that he kept in his wallet, unused. In fact, none of the guys, despite their boasting, actually used their extensive supplies for their intended purposes. Not yet men and no longer boys, they found it more fun to share them around, fill them with water and engage in water fights. Sometimes there were innocent victims, like the postmaster, who grew tired of picking up the condoms used in the water fights that often took place in the post office parking lot. He once caught them in the midst of a furious battle.

"Find somewhere else to play your idiotic games, and act your age!"

The boys departed but soon crept back, determined to pay him back for chasing them away. They opened the door to his always unlocked car, and placed on the back seat a condom, broken and watery after splattering on the post office wall. His wife, the malicious boys hoped, would find it when she cleaned her husband's car, blame him for infidelity, and exact their revenge.

The boy was careful never to use the condom his brother gave him for such childish pursuits – he was saving it for something more serious. From time to time, as coolly as he could, he would pull it out in the presence of the guys just to let them know he had one and was waiting for fate to deliver a willing partner. But destiny did not co-operate. Occasionally, he would look at it and think of what he could do if only a luscious high school girl came after him. He would resist her advances, of course, but only at first. Feeling sorry for her, he would magnanimously allow himself to be seduced.

The boy's imagination was further excited by the book he had taken. It was, in fact, not pornographic or even mildly suggestive. It was a colourful romance novel set in the antebellum South. But buried deep in the text was a line describing the arrival in New Orleans of a Mississippi paddlewheeler early in the nineteenth century.

"Voluptuous wenches lined the docks awaiting the disembarkation of the dissolute poker players."

That was enough to send the boy off into the realm of the most fantastic reveries. And he read and reread the passage until he almost wore out the page. Then one day, he heard his father ask his mother, "You haven't seen that book about life on the Mississippi, have you? I gotta return it to the library and can't seem to find it."

You mean the library actually loaned out books like that? The boy slipped into his parents' bedroom the next day and put the book back where he had found it. Then one day, he opened his wallet to show his parents how much money he had made that week delivering newspapers. The condom popped out and fell onto the floor. His parents were speechless.

"My brother gave it to me. I don't know what it's for! You kin have it! I gotta go!"

With that, the boy left the room.

His parents never mentioned the matter to him. But shortly thereafter, and perhaps just by sheer coincidence, the mother called the boy and his brother to join her at the kitchen table. Wearing a fixed smile, she opened a thick book borrowed from the library entitled

A Parent's Guide to Human Reproduction and proceeded to give a dry, analytical briefing, complete with highly fascinating diagrams, on the mating practices of sperm and eggs. The brothers could barely restrain their laughter. Their mother then solemnly dismissed her sons, their formal sexual education complete.

The boy was coming of age in more ways than one in the summer of 1953. The urge came upon him at that time to see what lay beyond the confines of his village and surrounding communities and to prepare himself to leave one day and live in the big city. Since his father neither owned a car nor knew how to drive, his family had found it hard to travel far from home since moving to Port Carling. Whenever the boy needed to make short trips outside the village, he fended for himself.

He would stand on the gravel road leading to the Muskoka Lakes Golf and Country Club, his thumb extended in the hope of being picked up by golfers travelling to the prestigious establishment. Around three in the afternoon, after putting in one or two rounds as a caddy on the eighteen-hole course, he would start walking home, hitching as he went, anxious to be on time to start his newspaper deliveries. When he wanted to see a movie in the nearby town, he would usually team up with his best friend. Experts in the art of hitching rides, they would position themselves at a good spot on the side of the highway near a crossroad where cars had to slow down, stick out their thumbs, and seek eye contact to entice drivers to pick them up. They had no trouble obtaining rides, and in that more innocent age, their parents never worried that they would come to harm, no matter how late they came home.

And they never did, although they had close calls. One night, the boy and his best friend climbed onto the back of a flatbed truck that stopped for them at the nearby town around eleven o'clock at night after the last show. It was dark and they did not see the drunken grins on the driver and his buddies crammed into the cab – and failed to notice the absence of racks along the sides of the back platform to prevent anyone sitting outside from falling off. Their backs against the cab, they braced their feet against the floor as the driver spun his tires on the pavement and took off with a rush. Giving no thought to his passengers, or perhaps forgetting they were even there, he careened around corners and smashed into potholes, jerking the boys from side to side and bouncing them into the air.

Approaching the first hill, the driver shifted gears and poured on the gas. The terrified youngsters, with nothing to cling to, began sliding backwards towards the rapidly retreating road. Desperately, they rolled over, stretched out their arms, and hugged the wooden bed of the truck. They were saved when the truck slowed during its ascent. The engine laboured, the roar from the muffler deepened, and the vehicle almost died as it approached the top. The boys scrambled back to their positions. But their troubles resumed as the truck began its descent on the other side. The driver shifted into high and put his foot to the floor, the sound of the tires on the asphalt changed from a rumble to a howl, and the old truck took off so fast it practically became airborne. And that was only the first hill.

The driver and his passengers in the cab, oblivious to the boys outside, partied away inside, singing country and western songs at the top of their lungs and taking quick pulls from a bottle of cheap overproof black rum that they passed back and forth, snorting and choking as the booze burned its way down their throats. Soon the befuddled driver aimed his vehicle at the white line and drove with abandon down the centre of the highway, pulling over to his own side with a laugh and a "Yee-haw" only when confronted with oncoming traffic. The nightmare journey was endless. Trailing oil and gasoline fumes, the old truck sped through moon-lit rock cuts, past telephone poles transformed into dimly visible crosses, into foggy low-lying swampy areas reeking of rotting vegetation, through swathes of bush that were blurs in the dark, and alongside fields of sweet-smelling fresh-cut hay.

In desperation, the boys dug their fingernails deep into the surface of the rough deck and hung on. Somehow they made it back to the village. Their legs numb and trembling from nervous exhaustion, they walked home silently, their fingernails torn and their hands filled with splinters. Just happy to be alive, the boy thought it best not to mention the matter to his mother. After all, many of the kids his age in the village got around in the same way and had similar adventures.

Trips to more distant places, however, were infrequent, and occurred only when his parents managed to talk someone with a vehicle into giving them a lift. When the travel was by car, there would be no room for the boy and his siblings, and they would stay at home. If the journey was by truck, they would climb into the box on the back, hang on to the racks, and have themselves a bouncing, fun, and windy ride. The highlight of these years was a trip over rough back roads to the circus in Parry Sound, on the shores of Georgian Bay. The boy was excited since his father had been telling his children for years that when he was a boy of thirteen, he had run off with a circus that was passing through his hometown. The experience was short-lived – his mother had tracked him down and dragged him home – but it provided sufficient fodder for him to recount story after story to his admiring children about the great time he had had and about the fascinating people he had met.

It was after dark when the driver of the old truck carrying the family pulled into the makeshift parking lot that was rapidly filling up with vehicles from communities throughout the districts of Parry Sound and Muskoka. The boy recognized and called out greetings to other kids from his village who were making their way with their families to the Big Top to take in the show.

Barkers called out to the crowd to hurry forward and buy their tickets while there was still time.

"Step right up! Step right up! Get them while they last! Come in and see the greatest show on earth!"

As the boy's mother slipped away to join the lineup, the father told anyone who would listen that he had once worked in a circus, had seen it all, and had only bothered to come to allow his children to have a good time. But when the boy's mother came back with the tickets, his smile could not have been broader, and he led the way enthusiastically through the crowd to their grandstand seats. The family huddled together, overwhelmed by the clamour of the crowd, as a brass band hammered out stirring tune after tune, and hawkers came down the aisles selling popcorn, peanuts, and cotton candy. The circus master entered the ring through a back entrance, snapped his whip, calmed the spectators, and announced that the official opening parade would begin.

To the delight of the audience, the retired heavyweight champion of the world, Joe Louis, entered riding a white stallion and leading a long train of circus performers and their animals. The crowd went wild, for Joe Louis was one of the most beloved and popular champions of all time, and boxing was a favourite sport of Canadians who tuned in faithfully on their radios every week to the "Friday Night Fights" sponsored by Gillette razor blades. What followed was anticlimactic, although the boy marvelled to see lions and their tamers, trick horses and their riders, clowns in all their varieties, dancing dogs, trapeze artists, elephants balancing on stools, and a man shot from a cannon into a net. And, country bumpkin that he was, he gawked unselfconsciously at a woman advertised as the fattest and hairiest in the world.

They also made trips southwards to the home of the boy's white grandparents – for wonderful, if sedate, family visits. Jaunts to the annual fall fair at his mother's reserve were infinitely more exciting. Drinking was officially banned there, but people had no trouble obtaining and consuming all they wanted. Fights would break out, usually with the boy's uncles in the thick of things, the RCMP would intervene, and a good brawling time would be had by all. Kids who spent their summers at the Indian Camp, and who were his buddies, would take him in hand and show him around, never forgetting to include the jail, which occasionally held a prisoner but was never guarded.

And from time to time, they visited friends who lived in a modest house close to Algonquin Park, some distance away. The good-natured, taciturn husband was a white man who scratched out a living as a part-time forest ranger and as a sculptor of animal carvings that he sold to tourists. The wife was an Indian from the mother's reserve and had been her closest friend since childhood. Like the boy's mother, she had been banished from the reserve when she married a white man.

Each spring, the mixed-race family would pay return visits, timed to coincide with the annual smelt run. For at that time of the year, after the snow had melted and the ice was gone from the lakes, the herring-like fish emerged from the rocky depths of the Muskoka Lakes to swim up the streams, rivulets, and rivers of the district in their millions to spawn. After dark, the men and boys of the two families would take their flashlights and homemade scoop nets, fashioned from mosquito screening, and join dozens of villagers in the shallows under the swing bridge over the Indian River.

Afterwards, when they brought home baskets of fish, the two mothers would roll the small, silvery catch in bread crumbs, flour, salt, pepper, and beaten eggs and fry them until they were brown and crisp. The two families would then "have a good feed" and talk late into the evening, the men in English with glasses of raisin wine and the women in Chippewa with cups of tea. The boy loved these encounters, since the children of the other family, like him, were rooted in two worlds, and he felt at ease with them.

Then one spring when the mixed-race family came for their visit, the husband was as cheerful as ever but his wife was more silent than usual and his children were quiet and withdrawn. It quickly became apparent that something was badly wrong. The ranger slurred his words, had difficulty in completing sentences, and from time to time, he would stop talking and stare blankly off into space. His wife took the boy's mother aside to say that her husband had been diagnosed with inoperable brain cancer and everyone was trying to make his last days as normal and enjoyable as possible. He died shortly thereafter. His wife defied the Indian agent and moved back to the reserve to live with her family, and the annual visits between the two families came to an end.

Then, in short order, the boy's white grandfather retired and moved with his wife to Port Carling. After that the boy's parents rarely left home and he grew frustrated. Books and radio and television programs had opened up a wider world to him, and he wanted to see it, particularly the big city of Toronto that he read about every day in the *Toronto Daily Star*. And each time he saw a train, he thought back to the trip he had taken with his grandfather toward the end of the war. In his imagination, he could still smell the odour of the coach they travelled on, see the towns and villages they passed through, remember the friendly bustle and excitement of Union Station, and recall the welcoming crowds on the main thoroughfares of the city itself.

Anxious to relive the experience, the boy quickly accepted when a neighbour invited him along on a daytrip to the big city. Climbing aboard the train at six in the morning at the nearest railway station, they entered a coach filled with sleeping passengers. The blinds were drawn, the interior was dark, and the smell within was of sweat, cigarette smoke, and air that had been breathed too many times by too many people over too long a period of time. The conductor roused a girl, about eighteen years old, who was slumped across three seats, shaking her gently and telling her that she had to make room for new passengers, before installing the boy and his companion beside her. She shook herself awake, sat up, and with a smile said something the boy did not understand.

"Tu ne parles pas le français alors?"

Seeing the boy's blank look, she switched to English.

"You don't speak French?"

It was the first time the boy had heard anyone speak French. The friendly girl told him that there was no work at home and she was going to Toronto in search of a job. Most of the people in the coach, she said, had boarded the train the previous evening in small towns in Northern Ontario and were also heading south looking for work. In short order, the occupants, roused from their sleep by the arrival of the newcomers, raised the blinds, opened the windows to let in fresh air, and filled the coach with the sounds of Canada's other official language. Soon a newsie selling magazines, newspapers, sandwiches, chocolate bars, potato chips, pop, hot water and tea bags, and weak coffee made his way down the aisle, peddling his wares. The boy listened to the animated, cheerful banter, a stranger in the midst of a people whose culture was new to him and who did not seem at all daunted by the prospect of leaving the comfort of their small communities to make new lives in the big city.

At first the boy enjoyed the journey. The sounds and smells of train travel were exactly as he remembered them. So too was the racing sun, this time at sunrise, that sailed behind telephone poles, trees, houses and barns. The steam locomotive chugged along through a familiar landscape, moving through pine, spruce, and maple forests, skirting cottage-fringed lakes, passing above rivers on trestled bridges, and after giving due warning with clanging bells and whistle blasts, gliding through railway crossings with their flashing warning lights. Every so often, it stopped to pick up passengers and freight at the blood-red railway stations that had been essential to village and town life in that part of Ontario for generations, before resuming its milk-run journey to the big city.

As the train entered heavily populated Southern Ontario, however, the boy began to feel uneasy. From the window, he saw the backside of Ontario – literally. The railway tracks ran behind houses and businesses, and in those days before people became conscious of the need to protect the environment, passengers were treated to candid views of the backyards of homes and businesses where litter lay uncollected, where weeds flourished, where householders let their grass remain uncut, and where business people neglected to paint walls or repair broken windows on the sides of their enterprises not facing the street.

When they entered the city, the boy's sense of disquiet increased, for it was not as he remembered. The train crawled over a surreal landscape dominated by factories, warehouses, and subdivisions stretching out mile after interminable mile and through enormous marshalling yards crowded with locomotives belching steam and being shunted from track to track. It was just too big and far from anything he had seen or experienced in his small-town Muskoka life for him to absorb. And at Union Station, instead of a friendly conductor providing helpful instructions as was the case when he was a little boy, railway employees herded the passengers like animals to slaughter through runways leading from the disembarkation platform to the main concourse. Later, in the downtown, instead of the welcoming wartime city of his memory, he encountered an impersonal, soulless metropolis where everyone was in a hurry, where the racket of honking car horns and clanging streetcar bells was overpowering, and where people moved like automatons through the streets at rhythms regulated by the flashing of traffic lights.

Had he, he wondered, just imagined his earlier visit to Toronto? Or had the passage of time transformed reality into romantic myth? Whatever the explanation, he was happy to return to the refuge of his Muskoka home, cured forever, he believed, of his desire to travel and to leave his small village for life in the big city.

Until that is, he encountered the tourist kid with an attitude. One day, while bagging groceries at Hanna's General Store, he helped a customer carry her purchases to her boat moored to the dock in front of Whiting's Drug Store and Ice Cream Parlour. A summer resident about his age, wearing fashionable aviator sunglasses and stripped to the waist to reveal his carefully cultivated golden tan, was driving around aimlessly in his outboard motorboat, showing off to a group of his friends lounging about on the docks. Seeing the boy looking at him, the youth cut the power to his motor, stood up, and yelled out.

"Whatcha looking at, you stupid hayseed? Haven't you ever seen an outboard motorboat before?"

His friends cheered enthusiastically, happy to see a local yokel put in his place. Restarting the motor, he then slipped the transmission into gear and ran his boat at full throttle at the boy, swerving aside at the last minute to slam the wake of his boat against the dock before taking off with a laugh and disappearing around the bend of the bay.

Out of incidents of this kind, revolutionaries are born. Words could not describe the loathing the boy felt at that moment for the pampered kid in the motorboat and his idle friends on the dock. Fury consumed him as he thought of the self-indulgent summer residents his age who spent their summers doing nothing in particular at their fancy cottages, driving expensive speedboats, and playing golf with Daddy and Mommy at the exclusive Muskoka Lakes Golf and Country Club while he and every other guy in the village had to work.

The boy did not become a revolutionary, but the episode that day made him resolve that a lifetime in the village was not for him. If the girl he met on the train could make a go of it in the big city, then so could a kid from Muskoka. He might even learn French.

FOURTEEN

—

The Father's Secret

In the summer of 1953, the boy as usual had continued to be keenly interested in life beyond the village as revealed through the pages of the *Toronto Daily Star*. "Uncle" Louis St. Laurent was prime minister. Winston Churchill, now an old man in his dotage, was once again leader of the United Kingdom. President Eisenhower, the great hero of the war, was the reassuring presence in the White House. And no longer did the news from Korea dominate the front page. The opposing sides had settled into an uneasy stalemate across the thirty-eighth parallel after communist and United Nations forces fought ugly see-saw battles for control of the Korean peninsula. There had been a flurry of press attention two years earlier when Canada sent the 25th Canadian Infantry Brigade to fight as part of the First Commonwealth Division in Korea. The troops performed valiantly, especially during the battle of Kapyong when a company commander of the Princess Patricias Canadian Light Infantry called supporting artillery fire down on his own position to drive off attacking Chinese and North Korean forces and save the day, but interest in Canada waned. By the time the formal ceasefire was signed in the summer of 1953, Korea had already become the forgotten war.

The boy was more interested in the recent death of King George VI and the coronation that year of Canada's new queen, Elizabeth II, at Westminster Abbey, amidst great pomp and ceremony. Special services were held at 9:00 a.m. on the day of the event itself at Anglican churches throughout Canada, including at St. James the Apostle Anglican Church in Port Carling, affectionately known locally as "the English Church." This was a time when the majority of Canadians were staunch and vociferous monarchists, when Canada did not have a flag of its own, when the Union Jack flew from flagpoles across the country, when most people sang *God Save the Queen* as their national anthem, and when the holiday message from the monarch was the highlight of Christmas morning.

And in those days there was not a stronger bastion of support for the Crown than the village of Port Carling, in particular the boy's elderly customers.

Anglican or not, they crowded into the English Church to mark the occasion. All agog at the coronation of the beautiful young princess, they infected the boy with their enthusiasm.

"Imagine! It took six Maids of Honour justa help her with her wedding dress! And didya see them Crown Jewels? And the four pairs of white stallions pulling her golden coronation coach! Ain't never been such a gatherin' of royalty, big shots, and world leaders!"

"Why, I kin remember when Edward VIII came to the throne. Seemed like a nice fella when he visited Canada as Prince of Wales. Whatta shame he preferred that woman Simpson to being king."

"That's nutt'n. I remember George V during the Great War."

"And me, I remember 'em all. George VI, Edward VIII, George V, Edward VII, and even Queen Victoria!"

Husbands and wives vied with each other in confirming their support for the Crown. Several had travelled to a railway station at a remote hamlet some thirty miles from Port Carling to wave to King George VI and Queen Elizabeth when they passed through the district in a royal train during the Royal Tour of 1939. With war expected to break out at any moment, the villagers had found it reassuring to be visited by their monarch and his wife in the troubled times. They had been deeply saddened when the King, who had become a symbol of wartime resistance despite being shy and speaking with a pronounced stutter, passed away the previous year. And so deep was their loyal affection, many could even remember exactly what they were doing when the news came of the passing of their monarchs over the past half-century.

The boy carefully stored away for his own grandchildren one day the special colour supplement put out by his newspaper and proudly told his customers how his Scottish grandfather, before he emigrated to Canada at the turn of the century, had often seen the old Queen. His family had run a shop selling groceries in the Highland village of Ballater and as a youngster he had made deliveries to the kitchen door of neighbouring Balmoral Castle, country home of the royal family. He thought it prudent not to mention the fact that his grandfather had in the interim become an ardent republican. And, rounding off the picture, he told them that his mother's side of the family was strongly loyalist, as were all native people who felt a historic link with the Crown that predated the official creation of Canada in 1867. A relation from the reserve had even been part of a group of pow-wow dancers who had entertained Queen Victoria at her London Diamond Jubilee celebrations in 1897.

The boy was happy to vaunt his family's monarchist connections because he was worried about a secret his father had told him.

"My boy, you're now thirteen and should be able to keep a secret. What I'm about to tell you I ain't never told nobody before, and you must keep it to yourself or I could go to jail. When I warn't much older than you are now, I was attracted by Marxism. In fact, a lot of the guys my age had given up on the system and believed the communists who held meetings in the union halls and made speeches on street corners. Our dads had been out of work for years, and we had no education and no hope. People today forget that in the Dirty Thirties the government was afraid of us and rounded us up by the thousands to send to remote work camps to keep us from demonstrating for our rights on the streets. When I was fifteen, I put in my time building roads for five dollars a month in Algonquin Park but left as soon as I could to go on the bum looking for a decent job. I was never a member of the Party, but for years, whenever I could, I sold copies of the communist newspaper on the streets. And when you were born, I named you James Karl in honour of Karl Marx. Of course I gave all that up years ago. I saw what Stalin did to his own people and to the Finns and to the Poles in 1939 and 1940 at the beginning of the war. Let's keep this our secret."

The boy was dismayed. For as long as he could remember, communists had been feared and reviled in Canada just as they had been in the United States. For Canada was still reeling from a world-class spy scandal that had badly damaged its national security and shocked the international community. In 1945, Igor Gouzenko, a cipher clerk working for Soviet military intelligence at the Soviet embassy in Ottawa, defected to the RCMP, carrying incriminating lists of Soviet agents and communist sympathizers in Canada. Canadians from coast to coast had felt betrayed by the actions of their wartime ally, and turned against the Soviet Union. And although eight years had gone by, the former spy appeared regularly on television, wearing a white hood to protect his identity, to denounce the Soviets and to keep alive the memory of communist duplicity.

Not a week went by without the press, especially magazines from south of the border such as *Time*, *Reader's Digest*, and *Life*, revealing further communist perfidies. More alarming still, anti-communist emotions were running at a fever pitch in the United States at this time. Joseph McCarthy, the Republican junior senator from Wisconsin, was alleging that the American State Department, the Voice of America, the movie industry, and even the United States Army were infiltrated by communists and was using his position as chair of the Subcommittee on Investigations of the

Senate Committee on Governmental Operations to root them out. No matter how far-fetched his accusations, many of the people he was identifying were being ostracized and driven from their jobs. Some were even taking their lives. And to make matters worse, the *Toronto Daily Star*, which was assiduously covering the McCarthy hearings, was reporting that the senator was even fingering Canadians.

Dismay turned to pride and then to fear in the boy. He was proud of his father for his noble principles and his efforts to do something to support them when he was just a teenager. But what would happen, he worried, should McCarthy find out that his father, a humble day labourer in the village of Port Carling, in the depths of the Great Depression had sold communist newspapers on the streets of a distant town? Would the infamous senator learn that the middle name of his thirteen-year-old son was Karl, after Karl Marx? Would he summon father and son to Washington to appear before his Senate committee and ask them to swear on the Bible that what they were about to say was the truth, the whole truth, and nothing but the truth? Would he ask them to state whether they were now or ever had been members of the Communist Party? Would McCarthy believe his father when he told them he had only sold the papers and had not been a member of the Party? Would he believe the son when he told them he had nothing to do with picking his middle name? Would father and son be condemned and sent to a secret American prison for communists?

Even without the McCarthy hysteria, it was a poor time for anyone in the village to be identified as a one-time Marxist sympathizer. The Cold War was raging. Canada had soldiers fighting the communists in Korea, and the Soviets had the atom bomb. Stalin had just died, but everyone expected that the new leaders, Nikita Khrushchev, Georgi Malenkov, and Nikolai Bulganin, would be no less hostile to the West. In school, teachers were conducting air-raid drills and telling students to duck under their desks and keep their backs to the flash when the warning sounded that Soviet bombers were overhead and about to drop the bomb on Port Carling. The old warriors down at the Legion had stopped exchanging stories about past wars and were focussing on the next, certain it would be just a matter of time before the Third World War began. The next generation, they said, would have to fight in Europe just as they had in 1914 and 1939. Several of the young men, who just five years earlier had led the Hallowe'en commando raid on the school toilet paper supplies, drew their own conclusions and joined up.

The boy was convinced that if anyone should learn of his father's former leftist leanings, his future would be ruined. He had already resolved that he would not spend the rest of his life in the village. Most of the people around him had been born in the village, would spend their lives working at the same job in the village, and would die in the village. Their lives might well be full and rich, but he wanted something more. He did not want to sleepwalk through life.

In grade eight, he had already gone further in school than his parents, and was a top student in his class. His father might have low expectations of his son, but his mother and his white grandfather were quietly encouraging. Relatives from his mother's reserve had also come calling at the old house and told him that no member of their family had reached grade eight, and said they were proud of him. He didn't want to let them down, and was determined to do his best in high school. If he managed to stay out of the way of the ruthless principal, he would have, he thought, a reasonable chance of obtaining his junior matriculation certificate and graduating from grade twelve. And afterwards, he told himself, he would take a two-month summer course to obtain a temporary teacher's certificate and find a position as a teacher for a year or two in a one-room school back in the bush where school boards could not attract properly qualified instructors. In that job, he would save his money and eventually go to university.

But now he thought his life was surely destroyed,

no matter what he tried to do or where he went. How could he ever explain to school boards, friends, and employers the origin of his middle name? As a half-breed, he already had one strike against him. Now he would be tarred with the same brush as a one-time communist sympathizer, even if he was his own father. All the progress his family had made in making friends and becoming accepted risked being for naught. At a minimum, the family would be shunned by the villagers, since there was not a more socially conservative place than Port Carling in all of the province. Even his best friend, he was convinced, would abandon him. And indeed, if somewhere and somehow he were to manage to become apprenticed to a carpenter, mechanic, or electrician, he sensed he did not have the aptitude to become a skilled tradesman. He feared that he would end up for the rest of his life in mind-numbing, poorly paid, and physically demanding dead-end jobs as a butcher's helper, like his friend, the former home boy, or as a casual labourer like his father, cutting grass, cleaning boats, working on construction sites, and cutting firewood for summer residents.

And that, he was convinced, would be the worst of all possible fates. His white grandparents had told him that their lives had been failures because of their lack of education. His grandmother's dream had been to be a doctor and she had been bitterly disappointed at having to leave school early to help out at home despite being academically gifted. The boy would often call on her in the small two-room retirement cabin she and her husband had built next to the old house. He would sometimes find her sitting before an old trunk where she kept her most precious possessions, nostalgically sifting through letters and photographs dating back to the end of the previous century from schoolmates less talented than she who had managed to continue in school and fulfill their destinies.

The boy's grandfather's story was one of great hope followed by great disappointment. In the spring of 1906, he had left his home in class-conscious Scotland, where employment prospects were poor, full of dreams for a better life in Canada, a mecca for young, unemployed Britons at the time. Almost half a century later, he could still remember every detail of the journey: how as a young man of twenty he had travelled from Aberdeen to Liverpool, how he had embarked on a passenger ship already filled with "Galician" farmers en route to Western Canada to take up homesteads, how the ship had pulled away from the dock with a blast of its whistle, and how the long voyage was made even longer by the need to navigate slowly through foggy, iceberg-filled waters off Newfoundland. He could still recall, he often told his grandson, how excited he had been at his first glimpse of Canada before his ship entered Halifax Harbour, the long ride to Toronto on a special immigrant train, and the frequent stops at small railway stations where he and his fellow immigrants were treated to buffet meals laid on by the railway of thick homemade bread covered by a generous coating of farmer's butter and thick slices of Argentinian bully beef, of the pitchers of fresh milk, coffee, and tea, and of the apple, raisin, and peach pies in profusion. And most of all, he would never forget the wonder and sense of new beginnings he felt as he looked out the windows of the train at his newly adopted country.

It had all been downhill from that time. To be sure, he had had his moments. The great passion of his life was socialism, and he had become a union shop steward, had supported a celebrated march of the unemployed on Ottawa during the depths of the Great Depression, and had used his talent as a public speaker to support left-wing candidates in election campaigns. He told his grandson, however, that he simply did not have the education to move up in the trade union world or to get a good job, had married too young, had too many children too soon, had become trapped in a cycle of poverty, and had never been able to realize the hopes he had when he left Scotland.

"Get an education, laddie, get out of this town and do the things your old granddad has been dreaming about all his life."

It would only be a matter of time, the boy was sure, before his father blurted out his secret. The boy was well aware that his father, in contrast to his own parents and his worry-wart son, never troubled himself about whether his life was or was not fulfilled. He just got on with life, and getting on with life for him was doing what he wanted to do and saying what he wanted to say, regardless of the consequences.

He could even imagine the scene. His father would be hosting a homebrew party back of the outhouse and everyone would be feeling good. He would, as usual, be providing his unbridled opinions on everything from religion to politics, to the superiority of raisin over dandelion or chokecherry wine, to the status of native people, and to blasting techniques in Muskoka granite. The others would be nodding their heads sympathetically while cheerfully telling him to shut up and pour them another drink. Someone would start to sing "Frankie and Johnny," and everyone would join in.

Johnny saw Frankie a comin'
Out the back door he did scoot.
But Frankie took aim with her pistol

An' the gun went roota-toot-toot.
He was her man, but he done her wrong!

To get their attention, his father would draw on his resources for inventive storytelling: "And by the way, I bet you guys didn't know I was once secretary-general of the Communist Party of Canada," or some such absurdity to get a laugh.

The boy's only hope was that his father's indiscretions on his politically incorrect past sympathies would pass over the heads of his drinking partners. They were not well-informed *Toronto Daily Star* readers, and at the best of times, only understood part of what their more learned host told them anyway. But he could not be certain.

FIFTEEN

—

Raisin Wine

The father's behaviour that summer did nothing to lessen his son's concern. Homebrew became his obsession, and he went on a veritable orgy of wine-making and drinking. He prepared crock after crock of raisin wine and drank some by himself, shared a great deal with his friends, destroyed an unknown quantity accidentally, and gave the rest away to strangers.

He was a driven man, he said, because the raisin wine of the summer of 1953 would rank among the top Muskoka *millésimes* of the century, and he had a duty to make as much of it as he could. He took special care in its preparation, using only the purest Muskoka rainwater channelled from the gutter off the tarpaper roof of the old house down a drainpipe into a battered black oak barrel infested with mosquito larvae and held together by rusty iron hoops.

The barrel had a history of its own. Charred on the inside to promote the aging process, its original purpose had been to transport dark brown overproof rum in bulk from Jamaica to Canada, where it was bottled and sold in government liquor stores. A summer resident had obtained one and brought it to his cottage, thinking he might cut it in two and use the halves as flower bins. The cottager abandoned his project and discarded the barrel at the dump, where the boy's resourceful father found it and brought it home. The great wines of Europe might capture their mouth-watering flavours from the ancient oak barrels in which they mature, but the father's wine received its special character – its *goût du terroir à la Muskoka* – from the *soupçon* of rum leaching from the scorched staves of the old rum barrel, together with the slight taste of tar in the rainwater from the roof.

Other elements, however, are also needed to make great wine and Port Carling's master wine maker knew them all. It was essential, he said, to replicate in the Muskoka bush the cool, somewhat humid but not overly moist conditions that exist in the ancient château cellars that produce the magnificent *grand cru* wines of the Burgundy and Bordeaux regions of France. And he did so by preparing his brew in a large crock of glazed earthenware that he buried almost up to its top in the dirt behind the outhouse under the shade of a sumach tree. This kept the brew exactly at the right temperature, neither too warm nor too cool, needed to produce *grand cru* wines in Muskoka. And the crock he used was not just any old crock. It was his pride and joy. He had craftily held back a portion of the weekly wages that he usually handed over on Saturday nights to his wife until he had saved nine dollars and ninety-nine cents. He then put the money in an envelope together with a letter written for him by his son and ordered it directly from a supplier advertising in the *Family Herald*.

Next, he visited Hanna's General Store to personally inspect its supplies of Italian raisins, Cuban sugar, and British yeast, selecting only the freshest and highest quality of these imported products. With his ingredients assembled, he took a tin pail and reverently filled the crock almost to the brim with his special water from the rain barrel. The raisins and the sugar he then delicately dumped into the water after blending them together in a large wooden bowl according to a secret formula. He then disappeared into the bush with a hatchet and re-emerged with a freshly cut branch from his favourite white birch tree and used it to stir the mix. For the desired effect, he said, it was important to ensure that the leaves were still on the branch.

In the particularly delicate part of the process that followed – one that set him apart from other Port Carling raisin wine makers – he gently settled a piece of toast, slightly burnt was the best, onto the surface of the liquid. On the toast he carefully placed a square of yeast. And just before the waterlogged toast with its load of yeast sank into the potion, he covered the crock with a tea towel and placed a piece of plywood on top. To keep out the raccoons, which in Muskoka had a fondness for raisin wine, he weighed down the plywood with a cement block. He then sat back and waited for his preparation to ferment.

Ten days later he removed the cement block, plywood, and tea towel and sampled his new elixir. The operation was not as simple as it might seem. Using a technique known only to master European wine makers, he sucked back the brew through open lips and closed teeth and gargled before swallowing. This strained out the swollen raisins, the undissolved bits of yeast, as well as the mosquito larvae, drowned ants, spiders and other insects, and parts thereof that had fallen into the brew. The sucking and gargling process also added the air to the wine that released its aromas to be captured by the olfactory nerve cells in his nose, which combined with the tactile feel of its unique texture on his palate to send a message of delight to his brain. He invariably judged his brew to be excellent and ready to drink. The outmoded practices of those who thought one should wait a few months or even years before imbibing were simply not for him. His wine, like a *beaujolais primeur*, was meant to be drunk while still young. In reality, it went bad after three weeks.

The final step was to pour the mix through cheesecloth into well-washed glass vinegar jugs, seal them tightly with corks, and store them under the stairs leading to the first-floor bedrooms of the old house. He then invited his friends over to drink and took a bottle with him when he went calling.

Some Muskoka wine-drinkers, not the true connoisseurs, of course, said his wine that summer was as watery and sappy as ever. These philistines even dared to say it smelled like an outhouse. However, those who really knew their wines could not find the words to describe it, declaring it to be youthful and aged, tight and loose, big and small, brawny and scrawny, crispy and wilting, smooth and rough, silky and coarse, ripe and green, raw and cooked, approachable and remote, spicy and bland, hot and cold, creamy and steely, understated and overstated, complex and simple, austere and luxurious, torpid and vigorous, and smoky and clear with intimations of sumach, oak, and cedar bark, light and dark chocolate, plummy and unripe fruit, saddle leather and sweaty horses, raspberries and blackberries, and oranges and grapefruits – all, of course, at the same time.

The father's raisin wine went well with all manner of dishes, whether as an aperitif with fish terrines and goat cheese or as an accompaniment to lamb, beef, roasted poultry or game. The consensus of the most discerning was, however, that it was really in its element when consumed with Muskoka culinary delights such as pork and beans, hot buttered toast, spicy pepperoni sausages, pickled eggs, and cold canned Bartlett pears. Some drinkers became ill after partaking, but everyone blamed that on a wave of stomach flu affecting the community that summer. All praised its high alcohol content and said a wine of such quality should be made available to the general public. They even had a name for it – "Muskoka's Own Kikapoo Joy Juice" – after the favourite drink of Pappy in *Li'l Abner*.

The boy's mother said nothing, not even when five jugs of wine, prematurely bottled and unable to contain the pressure of expanding carbon dioxide gas from the still fermenting juice, exploded one after the other, soaking the father's supplies of dynamite and nitroglycerine caps still stored in the same crawlspace, and blasting wine and broken glass out from under the stairs and across the downstairs room. For weeks, the house smelled of yeast, leading visitors to ask the mother if she was baking bread. She was mortified, but to the boy's father, it was just a big joke.

"Guess I'd better brew up another batch. This time I'll giv'er another day or two to let off the gas before the bottl'n."

She likewise said nothing when her husband went away for three days without telling her. Several good-natured members of the reprobate drinking class – the village druggist, a truck driver, and an auto mechanic – had dropped in late one night, and he had taken them and a jug of raisin wine to his favourite spot back of the outhouse to drink and tell stories. One of the company mentioned that he had a favourite sister he had not seen for years. She lived, he said, in far off Val-d'Or in the province of Quebec.

Raisin wine, as is well known, makes its drinkers philosophical, and the boy's father immediately made a proposal.

"Let's go see her right now. Life is too short. You may never see her again."

They thus departed for Val-d'Or, ten hours of hard driving to the north in the heart of Quebec's mining country, a jug of raisin wine concealed under the front seat. On arrival, the brother searched for her telephone number to call to tell her the happy news of their arrival. He then remembered her home was really in Dorval, just outside Montreal.

"Val-d'Or? Dorval? I always get them mixed up."

When she received the dishevelled band of hung-over travellers some eight hours later, the sister was very happy to see them. Coming from Port Carling herself, she understood the thinking of the locals and was not surprised they had taken the long way round to reach her. It took them another day to travel back to the safety of their Muskoka homes.

Then, one night – actually it was so late it was in the early hours of a Sunday morning – the boy's father went too far.

The boy and his brother were sleeping peacefully in their upstairs bedroom when they were awakened by their sisters crying and their mother screaming for their father. They became aware that someone was under their bed alternatively bellowing out curses and repeating in a low moan over and over again a heart-felt refrain.

"My best friend has betrayed me! My best friend has betrayed me! My best friend has betrayed me!"

The boy turned on his bedside lamp, looked down, and saw the head of Vern, his father's best friend, pop out from under the bed. Vern was blubbering tears of drunken self-pity, his eyes were wild, his face was contorted with rage, and his breath reeked of raisin wine. He had entered the family home undetected through the always unlocked front door, had come up the stairs, and had gone from bed to bed, crawling under each one in turn, screaming hysterically for the boy's father to "come out and fight like a man," terrifying the girls and upsetting the mother before ending up under the bed of the brothers, where he was apparently considering what to do next.

Seeing the two boys staring at him, Vern crawled out and sought to enroll them in his enterprise.

"Your dad was my best friend and he has betrayed me! You guys gotta help me find and kill him."

Without further elaboration and without waiting for an answer, he rose to his feet, took three giant strides to the top of the stairs, tumbled down the flight of steps, and gathered himself together at the bottom. He then sobbed out one last "my best friend has betrayed me," crashed through the front door, slammed the screen door behind him, and ran howling like a wolf and weeping uncontrollably down the street.

The boy's brother summed up the situation.

"Looks like Dad's latest batch was a good one. Now turn off the light. I wanna sleep."

The boy's mother came from her bedroom, reassured her daughters, and turned to her boys.

"What was that all about? And where is your father?"

The boy's brother turned his face to the wall and said nothing further. Outside, the malamute huskies barked and snarled. They knew something was wrong and wanted to be released from their chains to chase down the person who had violated the sanctity of their master's home. The boy's grandparents peered out of the kitchen window of their next-door cabin, anxious to know the cause of all the commotion.

Always ready for an adventure and his curiosity aroused, the boy took his flashlight and went in search of his father. He did not have to go far.

"Hey Jimmy! C'mon! C'mere! Over here!"

His father was hiding on the flat roof of the summer kitchen attached to the back of the old house.

"Vern's gone crazy. I don't know what's come over him. We were jus drink'n a little raisin wine in his liv'n room when he suddenly attacked me for no reason. I didn't want to hurt him and ran home to avoid a fight. He's gonna come back, but I'll be ready. You gotta climb up here and help me. We'll pull up the ladder, and when he finds us, he'll haffta stand on the water barrel and then climb up the drainpipe to get to us. We can jump him when he's crawl'n onto the roof and tie him up until he sobers up."

The boy suspected there was more to the story than that. His father fancied himself to be something of a ladies' man and must have done something to enrage Vern. The boy knew him well, having spent many evenings playing checkers and joking with him when he came with his wife to visit his parents. And the matter was no longer funny. While good-natured and full of humour when sober, Vern was the first to admit he became mean, unreasonable, and downright dangerous when drunk. He had even served time in prison. The boy took Vern at his word when he said he intended to kill his father. At the very least, he would badly beat him up in a drunken rage if he found him.

The worried boy left his father blabbering on about how, when, and where they could get the drop on Vern should he return, and went to talk to his mother. Distraught and deeply worried, she could give him no guidance on what to do. The boy decided to take matters into his own hands. He had no intention of hiding with his father and becoming involved in a fight on a roof from which everyone could fall off. Something had to be done, however, and he was determined he would not allow Vern to harm his father and frighten his mother and sisters again. His family had no telephone, and he couldn't telephone Old Jack for help. He assumed that Old Jack, in any case, would be no match for Vern and could even get hurt if he intervened.

Displaying a monumental lack of judgment, the boy then went to the gun rack on the wall, took his .22 rifle down, dusted it off, and went in search of the special solid point ammunition that he had used to knock porcupines out of the tops of tall spruce trees when he still hunted. He loaded the gun, went down the path to the bottom of the steps leading from the old house to the highway, and waited.

As he stood there in the early morning chill, he remembered that it was at this exact spot, under the wild cherry tree, where he had mutely greeted Canada's figure-skating heroine, Barbara Ann Scott, who had come in search of bait worms in the summer of 1949, in vain. Although only four years had gone by, an eternity had passed. The boy now felt his boyhood was definitely over and he prepared himself to face the greatest test of his life.

And the climax of the night's nonsense was at hand. From afar, the boy could hear the sound of fire alarms clanging in the Port Carling House, the stately if somewhat seedy old hotel that had graced the downtown business section for more than seventy-five years and had escaped the great fire of 1931. The boy assumed that Vern was in the hotel sowing panic among the guests, who were setting off the fire alarms in the hope help would arrive soon.

The boy knew the hotel well since he cut the lawn for fifty cents once a week and had the run of the place. The elderly guests, he was well aware, were creatures of habit and would have gone to bed shortly after dinner on Saturday night, expecting to waken to the sounds of birds quietly chirping and of church bells gently pealing, calling the faithful to worship at one of the three churches in the village. After all, they had been coming, year after year, and generation after generation to Port Carling to enjoy the good Muskoka air and the quiet pleasures and comforts of summer life in what, until that night in any case, was arguably the most peaceful, dry, moralistic, respectable, virtuous, conservative, churchgoing, and welcoming small tourist community in all Ontario – if not in all Canada, or for that matter in the entire British Empire.

And they loved the Port Carling House with its wide verandahs screened to keep out mosquitoes and black flies, its antique wicker furniture, its elegant overhead fans, its copies of the *Toronto Daily Star*, the *Toronto Telegram*, and the *Globe and Mail*, its collection of ancient and dusty *Ellery Queen* detective stories, its two-year-old *Reader's Digests*, *Time* magazines, *Colliers* and *Maclean's*, its dog-eared playing cards and its cribbage boards. They loved its spacious and finely mown lawns, its croquet sets and its Muskoka chairs, strategically placed overlooking the locks to allow the guests to relax comfortably while watching the steamboats and their passengers come and go. They loved the polite Scottish-Irish-English locals who were infused with stalwart WASP values and who greeted them respectfully when they took their daily constitutional walks around the village. But most of all, they loved the fine, mouth-watering cuisine of the old hotel, especially the meat dishes prepared each day by Eva the cook, who had worked at the hotel for the past fifty years and who was looked upon by the regulars as a sort of mother figure.

The guests, however, did not know the secret behind the Port Carling House's culinary success. They did not know that the old hotel was owned by the butcher who spat on the floor when no one was looking and who held court with his alcoholic buddies behind the meat freezer of his shop on Friday nights. They were unaware that for years, to cut back on food costs in the Port Carling House, he had been providing Eva with chickens and roasts of beef so black and mouldy and with slabs of bacon so green with age that he could not sell them in his shop. All the unsuspecting clientele knew was that the meat dishes on every menu were so tender, they practically disintegrated as they forked them into their mouths. They raved in particular about the Chicken Fricassee, the highlight of the gastronomical week, served every Sunday evening. The best Chicken Fricassee, everyone knows, is made by taking a seasoned chicken, browning it slowly on all sides until well done and then removing the bones and adding the meat to a mixture of slowly cooking rice and onions in a flour-based sauce. Eva's chicken was brown inside as well as out – and the guests could not get enough of it. And the smell of it cooking – well, it had to be experienced to be believed.

The secret was, of course, known to the villagers, but they saw no reason to enlighten the guests and thereby spoil the enjoyment of their meals. Besides, they did not want to discourage them from spreading the word that the dining room of the Port Carling House was one of Muskoka's greatest assets – so good, they said, it would rate three stars in the Michelin culinary guide if only the snobbish French arbiter of culinary excellence knew it existed.

Time passed, and the boy shifted his weight from foot to foot. In the meantime, the fire alarms maintained their relentless appeal for help but the village volunteer firemen, reluctant to get out of bed and perhaps hoping the call for help was only a false alarm, were nowhere to be seen. The old guests were being abandoned to their fate, it seemed, but the boy didn't worry about them, finding their predicament ludicrous and even funny. Besides, he had his own problems. Vern, he expected, would soon return to conduct a more thorough search of the old house, and although he was only a kid, he would have to deal with him.

Sure enough, he saw the silhouette of a figure under a streetlight off in the distance coming from uptown making his way in his direction. Thinking it was Vern, the boy slid a bullet into the chamber of his gun, pushed off the safety catch with his thumb, and stepped out onto the highway. He intended to challenge him and drive him away from his home whatever the cost. To his immense relief, Old Jack hove into view, walking slowly.

The constable glanced at the gun and stood quietly beside the boy for a minute before starting to chuckle.

"Seems your dad and Vern have caused a bit of trouble tonight. Vern's running through the hotel looking under the beds for him, and the guests have pulled the fire alarms."

He hitched up his pants and chuckled again.

"Greatest excitement in the old hotel since the great fire. Those old maids and retired parsons are huddled together in their bathrobes out on the front lawn all a-twitter. I tracked Vern down, but he won't stand still or listen to reason. Says he saw your dad messing around with his wife and is convinced he's hiding in one of the bedrooms of the old hotel. He's going from room to room crawling under the beds and running aimlessly up and down the halls crying out his best friend has betrayed him and he's gonna kill him. I can't get him to listen to reason and have called for backup from the Provincial Police."

The boy said his father was hiding on the back roof.

"A good place for him to be for the time being. And by the way, Jimmy, don't worry about Vern coming back here tonight. You can put that gun away. Everything's now under control, and you might shoot someone, even if in self-defence, and regret it for the rest of your life. G'nite, son."

The next day, the Provincial Police from the nearby town who had locked Vern in their cells for the night to cool off released him. The boy's father and Vern shook hands, laughed, and were friends once again.

The mother, less forgiving, had a heart-to-heart talk with her rueful husband, who vowed insincerely to behave himself in future. She then went to the woodshed, grabbed an axe, and smashed to pieces his expensive glazed earthenware crock. Thus ended the boy's father's wine-making activities and the wild parties out behind the outhouse – for the time being, in any case.

Epilogue

THE FATHER WOULD TAKE HIS political secret to the grave, and the boy would realize his dreams. A wealthy American summer resident would befriend him and fund his university education. His life would turn out to be just as exciting as those he had read about in the comic books he devoured as a boy, and even more wonderful than the magical world he had glimpsed in his youthful and overactive daydreaming. He would join Canada's Foreign Service, have run-ins with bandits, spend time with Indians in the jungles of Latin America who still lived a pre-Columbian way of life, survive earthquakes, witness civil strife, help combat the world's last smallpox epidemic, meet people so wretchedly poor their living conditions defied the imagination or so rich their excesses were grotesque, become ambassador and adviser to foreign ministers and prime ministers, encounter many of the world leaders who shaped the latter half of the twentieth century, serve his country as a diplomat on all six habitable continents in a career lasting more than thirty-five years before going on to represent the Crown in his home province. At one time during the Cold War, he would even assume responsibility for the security desk in Foreign Affairs and work closely with the RCMP, which was unaware of the origin of his middle name, in helping defend Canada against attempts by the former Soviet Union's notorious KGB to recruit Canadian diplomats to spy for it.

In all these years, he would never lose his attachment to the village of his youth. In far-off places as different from one another as the swamps of Bangladesh, the mountains of Colombia, the highlands of South Africa and Australia, the deserts of Israel and Namibia, the urban wastelands of New York City, and the rainy capital of Belgium, he thought often of his boyhood years in Muskoka when the Great Depression had just ended, when the Indians came back in the summers to the Indian Camp, when there was regular steamboat mail and passenger service on the lakes, when the veterans of the two world wars were still young, and when there were locals still alive who remembered the pioneer days.

He reflected on how fortunate he had been to have such caring parents and grandparents, to have roots in the native and non-native worlds, to have been raised in a village with an excellent library, and to grow up among people, who despite reflecting the social and racial intolerance of the times, understood his idiosyncrasies, and were supportive when he sought an education.

And half a century later, the boy, now white-haired and long-retired, took as much pleasure in telling his children the stories of his early years in Muskoka as his father had in describing his youthful adventures to his kids when they lived in the old house. He told them, however, that he had been incredibly lucky. He had not hurt anyone when he acted out his wild fantasies laying ice cream cone spikes on the highway and sabotaging truck tires when he was barely out of childhood in 1948. He had escaped a beating at the hands of the drunken trucker in the summer of 1950. He had not fallen off the speeding truck, and he had shot no one when he foolishly armed himself with a .22 rifle to protect his father in the summer of 1953.

He also thought of the questions that he had first started asking himself at the time of his Muskoka boyhood. Looking back, he saw that all he knew about God was that he still did not know him – though he continued to search for him in the wind. All he knew about time was that a lifetime of experience merely confirmed his intuition as a child – that all living things change and pass away in its embrace, and eternity was a concept he would never grasp. All he learned about death was that consciousness was its twin – that death gave meaning to life, and consciousness was a gift that came but rarely, but when it did, it made life worth living. And all he knew about wisdom he had learned from his father – embrace nature and laugh, laugh, and laugh again at the joys and absurdities of life.

Also by James Bartleman

Out of Muskoka (2002)
On Six Continents (2004)
Rollercoaster (2005)